My Life Story

A Series of Little Miracles

To Saul Rivera

From James Roberts

Your friend

In Christ

God Bless You

James Roberts

Photo: Greenwood Lake, MI. by Peter Hall

To you,

   Thank you for taking the time to read about my journey with our Father through this glorious adventure of life. I have been greatly blessed with two outstanding women, who have allowed me to love them, care for them, and to call them wife. I have incredible children, grandchildren, and even great-grandchildren. I am very grateful to my dear friend Kathy Goldring for taking the time to listen to my story, and sort through all of my papers, to put this story together for me. I can never thank you enough for transcribing all of this for me. I am also grateful to my grandson Rich McDowell for taking the time to conduct the final edits for me on this piece of work. I hope that I have done more good in this life than not, and trust that our Father will greet me with opens arms when my time has come. Until we meet again...

James Roberts
1545 W. Grovers Ave
Phoenix, AZ 85023

Transcription: Kathy Goldring at KatGoldring@aol.com
Final Editing: Rich McDowell II at rmcdowell18@cox.net

"Oh, I don't worry nothin' 'bout that sort of thing, I just trust the Lord to protect me..."

- James Roberts -

Prologue

My life could have been very different from what it was. Through all of my adventures, mishaps, losses, and gains; the Lord has never left my side. I have overcome great struggles, persevered through tragedy, and shared in the love and kindness of good people along the way. Hopefully you will see the series of little miracles all throughout my life, just as I have come to see them. This is an unfiltered look at the journey I've been on, told in my own words, and from my perspective. I've done my very best to be honest, thorough, and to give God the credit where He is due.

Chapter 1

My name is James Roberts. I was born in 1941 in Greenwood, Mississippi. I'm one of five kids. My parents married on November 22 in 1926. My dad, James Emmett Roberts, was born in Springfield, Illinois on July 10, 1904. My mother, Rosa Licinda (Lamb) Thunderburk Roberts, was born January 29, 1900 in Red River County, Texas. She was married once before to a man named Thunderburk before she married my dad. She died in August, 1953.

My grandpa, James Henry Roberts, was born in 1855 and died in 1940 before I was born. My grandmother, lda, was full blood French. My older sister, Rosie Marie, was born on February 4, 1928. My second sister, Claudia Lee Roberts was born June 17, 1933. My third sister, Emmittine, born in 1935 or 1936, didn't live very long after her birth. Then there was James Emmett Roberts, Jr., born March 8, 1938. He had an enlarged heart and lived only three months.

Then I was born in 1941 in Greenwood, Mississippi. There's just me and my sister left out of those five kids. Guess, I could count my very existence as one of the great miracles in a lifetime of wonderful blessings and miracles. My parents lived in hard times when mortality rates were high, but I was one of the survivors of those difficult times.

It takes courage
to grow up and
become who you
really are
e.e. cummings

Got to say a word here about all these family names, so family after me can sort them out.

Grandfather: James Henry Roberts
My father: James Emmitt Roberts
Me: James Fred Roberts
My brother: James Emmitt Roberts (Jr.?)
Cousin: James Howard Roberts
Father-in-law: James Thomas Warren Smith
Son-in-law: James Hartsock
Grandson: Desmond James Bangura
Great Grandson: James Reed Lakomski
Grandson: Donald Ray Goin, Jr. (Ducky Duck/Ducky)
Granddaughter: Tina (Tina Weenie when she was 6)

So, I didn't know too much about my grandpa. He was born about 1865 and died in 1940 in Mississippi. He was a butcher by trade. I don't know if all the story is true on him or not, but he was quite an old codger. He was, well, some of the story on him is that he made the moonshine. He was very cruel. He'd hit my dad in the nose until he bled. No one had any good to say about Grandpa. He wouldn't tell you but one time to get up. The next time you were on the floor. One story was my dad went swimming, and grandpa caught him and whipped him all the way home naked. He had a brother, East Roberts, that I know about, and he was younger than my dad, and if there was any kind of work, my uncle was always too sick. Grandpa would let him stay home. My dad would go out and help Grandpa. As soon as the younger brother would see dad and Grandpa come in from the field, he would be okay.

One of the stories on Grandpa is that he loved to play the fiddle. Anyway you wanted it played-upside down, between the legs, it didn't make no difference to grandpa. He played at barn dances and stuff like that.

Now one of my sisters was going to be born, and he was going out there to watch her being born and my aunt, my mother's sister, said, "No, you're not."

She took off her shoe and was going to hit him with it. My dad said, "If you're going to hit him, you'd better hit him good." But grandpa went on out to the barn. He didn't see the baby born. Guess my aunt won that argument. Maybe that shoe worked.

And then one time, my mother and my grandpa was talking. He said something about one of my aunts. I think it was my Aunt Cordie. And my mother had just gotten back from getting water, and she threw the water on my grandpa. My dad didn't hit her. He just shook her and told her, "Don't never do that again to my Dad."

Grandpa was a butcher by trade, and he'd kill a goat or sheep or something, and he run out and get a cup and drink the blood off of it. One of the stories was that when he was a young man, he followed the harvest crew around.

At one place they stopped at they seen an old dog that came up for scraps at meals. At supper, they went in and had dinner and wondered where that old hound was. Turned out that dog was their dinner. A whole bunch of them got sick.

I never did know Grandpa, just heard references about him. Never heard no good about that old man. Mean and drunk. So, maybe that not knowing him and having to suffer through his tyranny was another blessing in my life. Just hearing about him was bad enough.

My Mama met my Daddy at a barn dance. She got a divorce from her first husband who'd bitten her on the hand. She slapped him, and that was that.
She was four-and-a-half years older than my Dad. That was my Dad's first marriage.

I had a picture of my dad, my mother and Claudia Lee, and he was saying, "The sun won't come down 'til I will kill that hog," or something like that.

Being drunk once, Dad got his leg broke. He was driving a logging truck in Mississippi while he was drunk. He turned the truck over; a log fell on him and broke his leg. One time Dad called a doctor who came out to the house. He chewed my Mama and my Dad out and said next time he did something so stupid not to call him. He wouldn't come again. He'd just send a little black wagon to carry the body down to the graveyard and throw Dad in. Guess my Daddy took him serious, because my Daddy quit drinking.

One time I heard stories about when my mother locked him out when he'd come home drunk from drinking eggnog, so he stayed outside all night. Then there were rumors going around that my Dad was seeing other women. My mother found out about it, and she had a gun in one hand and a knife in the other. She caught Dad with some woman. My Dad talked her out of harming them. I never asked Dad about it. He was the type of person that if I'd asked, he'd have told me it was none of my business. Period.

They were married in 1926. It was about twenty-five years or so. They came out to Texas in 1944 in August. That was a small miracle-that moving out to Texas-because I met with folks there that changed my life for the good. Guess, by then I must have had a guardian angel watching over me.

And so we lived in FortWorth until about 1971, somewhere around in there. I remember we had a two-room house. We had a living room-bedroom combination and a kitchen. We didn't have no inside toilet, just an outhouse. To keep warm in the wintertime, we had a kerosene burner and flatirons. We'd heat those flat irons up, wrap them in paper and put them in bed with us. That would keep us warm, and then we'd have blankets on top.

We had an old icebox. We'd put the sign out when we needed it filled. The iceman would bring the ice in and put the ice in the icebox for us. We had a well at one time. Daddy covered it up, but later cleaned it out, and we used that water to irrigate the garden. He covered it back up again when we quit using it.

I remember one Christmas Eve my dad worked at a service station at night. I fell asleep one night, and when I woke up I had a little red wagon that my Dad got me. And in Texas they called a group of kind people Good Fellows, and they would bring your Christmas presents to you, or you could go in and get them. I know now what a great organization that is, and how all those people were blessings to lots of kids, not just me and my sister.

I don't know how true this was, but my family said when I was a baby, I'd put the dog's tail in my mouth and bite it. Must have been a small miracle in there somewhere, 'cause most dogs would've bitten back, but I was fine. I was Mama's baby, but Daddy was the boss. Mama wouldn't go out and get anything without Daddy buying it for her. So, my Dad had the final say-so.

A is for always thinking of others
N is for numerous kind acts
G is for going above and beyond
E is for endless devotion
L is for how much you are loved !

I remember my Mama was always sick and went to the nursing home because my Dad couldn't take care of her. My aunt would come by. One day my older sister left home and went to live with my aunt. Whenever I got home from school my Dad said, "Well, your sister's gone. Your aunt chewed me out, and they left."

My Mama was still sick. She came back home for a time, and my uncle and aunt moved in, and they helped take care of my mother. They had a trailer that they moved in on our lot beside the house.

I was about eleven years old when my mother passed away. She died in the nursing home in 1953. That was tough going for a while. Not a blessing as far as I was concerned at that age. I'd been told she'd gone on up above, but that didn't mean nothing to me at that time. It was hard not having her.

When I was in the first grade, I'd do everything that teacher told me to do except for one thing. I wouldn't read for her. I thought like my Dad, and I didn't think a woman should tell boys or men what to do. That teacher would whip my hand every day I went to school. Every day, she'd ask me to read or what the story was. I'd say, "I don't know," and she'd whip my hand.

Or I'd mess my clothes, and the teacher would call in my sister who was in the seventh grade to come pick me up and take me home. They should have failed me that year, but they didn't. She didn't want to get me again, I guess. So, there was a little miracle that I was passed on and not held back. Might have been a special miracle and blessing for that teacher, too.

They passed me every year until I got in the seventh grade, and then they forgot to pass me! Oh, that was a shock. I'd never failed a grade before, and I had to tell my Dad. I just knew my Dad was gonna whip me, but . . . he didn't! Now, I had witnessed a miracle for real! He did not whip me!!

He just patted me on the head and said, "That's okay, son. If you want to stay in the seventh grade until you're twenty-one, fine. But you will go to school every day, and you will behave yourself. I'll make sure of that, even if I have to kick you in the pants down the road, I'll do that. I can't make you learn, but I can make you go to school". I knew my Dad meant it, so . . . if it hadn't been for my Dad in the seventh grade I would have quit. So I went on ahead and finished school. Guess God can work in strange ways. A threatened kick in the rear is what it took for me to keep on with my education. And that education served a great benefit and blessing as I went through life.

Me and my older sister got ornery and mean once, and she wouldn't let me ride her bicycle. So I grabbed the handles and pulled her into a ditch. 'Course, she'd tell Daddy on me, and I'd get a whippin'. Yeah, I did. I deserved it, though.

When my mother passed away, my Dad met another lady. They got married in 1954, I think it was. She had five kids already, because she'd been married three times before. My Dad was her fourth husband. Before they were married, she saw him going down the road with another lady one time, but I guess nothing came of it. However, before my mother passed away, and he'd met this lady he married, there had been another woman. She was a big ol' heavyset woman. My step-mother, at the time, was renting a place from that lady. And this heavyset woman had a crush on my Dad. So she told my soon-to-be step-mother that she was gonna whip her. My step-mother wasn't gonna take that. That renter lady had a daughter, and that daughter was mean.

One night that daughter's father was taking a shower, and she cut the army blanket. But she didn't get in no trouble for it. She threw a rock at my step-brother one time. My step-sister and future husband knew her. This mean girl would follow him home. He'd tell his mother, "Make her go on home." Her name was Thelma.

After my Daddy married my step-mother, we lived in a trailer for a while. And then my step-brother built a little house out there, and my step-mother and I used that as our bedroom. Came a time when I got my motorcycle license. I had to go up there three times to take the test. Three times for the written and three times for the driving. The first time I failed the driving test on the motorcycle. I was told to turn right. I turned left. The second time, I went all the way around. There were stop signs, so I slowed down, but I didn't stop. So, I failed it again. Third time came. The motorcycle would barely run uphill. You could walk up the hill faster than that motorcycle. I passed it that third time and got my license. Strange miracle, that one was.

The motorcycle belonged to me and my step-brother. I didn't ride it very often, because I could never get it started. I'd kick and kick and kick. He'd kick it one time, and off he would go. And when I did drive it, I'd see the stop sign, but couldn't get it to stop and ran right across it. My step-brother wouldn't let me ride it no more with him on it.

One time the motorcycle broke down, and my Dad was gonna pull me home with a chain. The chain popped. I went flying out in mid-air and landed on my knees. By the time the man following us got over to us, he was yelling,

"Are you hurt, sonny?"

"No. I'm just bruised up."

Small blessing there. I could really have been busted up badly, but l was all right. He chewed out my Dad. So Dad took me on home, left the bike, went and got my step-brother and pulled him home on the bike.

My step-sister was about twelve years old. She cooked pinto beans. Her step-sister's boyfriend told her if she put "Blueing" in them, that when people broke wind, you could see the "blue." So, she followed his instructions. We all ate that big ol' pot of beans. Then she told us she had put blueing in it. We threw the rest of the pot away, and didn't eat no more of those. Don't think any of us saw "blue fumes." But, it might have been a small miracle that none of us ended up in the emergency room with some kind of poisoning!

In high school I was in the NCC (National Cadet Corp). I was a private first class... uh, no... buck private... and I made private first class by selling peanut brittle candy. One day I was going by the grocery store and had that peanut brittle with me. And those people thought that I had stolen it. They questioned me, and they ended up buying a bag of it. After they questioned

SCHOOL DAYS 1958-59
BIRDVILLE

me, I hitchhiked to work. My Dad was told what happened. It made him mad. He knew I was honest.

On the rifle range, I would shoot the target okay. Trouble was, it wasn't my target which I did aim at. I'd end up hitting someone else's target. So, I didn't get any medals for my target shooting. Considering my bad aim, guess it was somewhat of a small miracle I didn't shoot someone!

The next year they put me in the DECA program which allowed me to work in the afternoon after school. I worked for James Beloate at Beloate Trim Shop for four years.

His son was my seventh-grade PE teacher. And his son moved up to Alaska to teach and wrote to his dad, saying," Those Texas boys were sissies, and those Alaskan boys were men."

When I had him for a PE teacher, he'd make us go out on the coldest days, when goosebumps were on our legs and he'd tell us, "Run, run, run! Let's move, move!"

I worked for Mr. Beloate for a long, long time. He was a real nice man. He put up with me, even though I could never operate a sewing machine. It'd run away with me!

I had a girlfriend in my junior year. We went out on several dates. I was apparently too tame for her. She wanted someone wilder than I was. That junior year, in April, my Dad died. That made me more determined to graduate. And I did graduate. I did. I even went to the cemetery and showed my Dad my diploma. Guess that was a really big miracle in my life. My Dad was a lot responsible for my achieving that diploma.

Then Mr. Beloate knew a man in Texas Rehab. He told Texas Rehab folks about my case, and about me wanting to go to school. I went to night school.

My stepmother moved to Decatur, Texas. Her daughter was there. The daughter had a rough life. Her first husband accused her of being crazy, but she wasn't. She had a little boy. And her husband got custody because of the things he said about her.

She met another man. He was abusive to her and beat her. She met her third husband, Ray. Ray hit my stepmother once when she went out to protect her daughter. My stepbrother went out with a two-by-four and knocked him in the head and stopped Ray. Knocked him down. He never did get drunk anymore and beat her up, as far as I know.

When my Dad died, after I graduated, we went to Decatur, Texas. I graduated on June 4, 1961. I didn't have anywhere else to go. I shoveled corn out of a trailer and helped my brother-in-law with the hay baling. He was a trucker that hauled hay for a living.

Mr.Douglas of Texas Rehab came down and told me he would pay me to go back to school if I would go back to school. He would do that if I had someone to live with. I called up my Aunt and she said, "Yes."

So I lived with her. We picked peanuts and picked up pecans to make ends meet. We sold them. I did this work while going to school. I had my junior accounting diploma in about three months. I didn't realize then, what a great achievement that was, but it became a turning point in my life; a true miracle that set me on a stable path to earn a living for myself and my family, and without having to pick up pecans.

However, the peanut and pecan picking was not my first time to work. Before I'd lived with my aunt, I had plenty of opportunity to work and took some of that opportunity to get into some boyhood scrapes. Yes, I did.

Back when I was about twelve or thirteen years old, I sold donuts. Me and my step-brother had a donut route. We would ride over to where Dad worked, and Dad would bring us home. When we quit doing that, Dad had us working at the service station with him.

One time me and my step-brother were in a department store to get some poker cards. He was going to take them. I waited for him. He ran out and said, "Go! Go!" The store detective caught us and questioned us. My step-brother wouldn't tell the detective anything, but I told them my life history. I was scared of the law, and thought they knew everything anyway.

So, the detective let us go and we got back to the service station, and we didn't say a word. Dad never did know about that. Now, there was definitely an angel nearby with that blessing!

And one time me and my brother David went out drinking. We had a contest about who could drink the beer the fastest. I think I won because I got drunk. I couldn't stand up straight. I went home, and my step-mother was fussing at me and my half-sister was, too. Both of them were giving me a fit. All because I went in the house and fell down and rolled on the floor. They held a cold cloth to David's head, and they were saying, "Poor David. Poor David."

They forgot to holler, "Poor James. Poor James."
I passed out on the floor, but when somebody poured cold water over me, I was awake and ready to party again! When I got into bed, my David knocked me off, but I got back on

the bed. Elaine said, "He ain't gonna quit trying. May as well let him lay."

Then David went out to the car and threw up. So, that was one time I really got lit. Nothing miraculous happened that time, and I suppose I didn't deserve it, acting that way. Generally speaking, I didn't do that often.

One time after my stepbrother got his driver's license, he had an accident. I was with him. He was picking up our half-sister from school, and she was in about the first grade. Just then, a little three-year-old girl, playing in the ditch, ran out in front of us. They had to give him a shot and knock him out. My stepmother said she was glad I had been with him, because he had a reputation of being wild, and I had a reputation of being calm. I think that accident was one reason he became an alcoholic. He never got over that accident.

Now back to my Aunt Claudia. When she came to our house, my older sister and me would clean up our house. I still hated for women to tell me what to do. One time when I was doing something I wasn't supposed to be doing, my aunt was gonna whip me. My Dad wasn't working that night. So, I ran in my Dad's bedroom and hid behind him. 'Cause she couldn't get me there. I'd be safe. Well, she came and pulled me out. And Dad didn't protect his son. He let her take me for a whipping!

I had another aunt, Aunt Cordie, who lived in Bandera, Texas. I went to visit her one summer. She liked me, but she couldn't stand my sister. My sister got pregnant by her uncle, and my Dad knew it. He warned my aunt, but she'd just say, "No, no. Woody would never do such a thing."

Then when he got drunk and did get my sister pregnant, my aunt wanted a divorce. Uncle Woody said, "If you divorce me, I'm not gonna marry her, anyway."

So my aunt decided to stay with him, and they raised the baby. And my sister could see the baby anytime. That went on for a little while until my sister met a man and married him.

Now, while living with my aunt in Fort Worth, I got my driver's license. She had gave me driving lessons. No one else would do it. Not my Dad. Not my step-brother. No one wanted to get in the car with me driving. I remember one time I was going really slow to get on the road. She'd told me to count the wheel. Then a pickup comes up fast as I'm finally easing onto the highway, and she yells, "Giddy up, James, giddy up." So, I did, but the pickup had to swirl around and it turned in a circle. My aunt never told me to "giddy up" again. Small miracle that truck missed me. That time.

One time in a parking lot, she was hitting me over the head with her shoe. So I went between two parked cars. I shouldn't have, but I did. I had to go three times to take my written test. And then that third time, I had to take the driving part, finally. They told me to parallel park. I didn't know what they were talking about. Parallel park? So . . . I had to go back three times to take the driving part and finally passed. Now, I could drive myself back and forth to work. That was a blessing. Not sure if it was such a blessing for the other drivers on the road, but I was happy about being able to drive!

I went to work at Palmer Upholstery Shop. I knew him from before when I was selling donuts. I'd met him then. I was working on the upholstery on a car top. I tore it all apart and threw it in the trash can. Uh-oh. He made me crawl in that trashcan and get all of that torn-up upholstery out. We had to use that to make a pattern.

My stepmother did not like my boss at Palmer Upholstery because my brother had worked for him and fired him. My stepmother stayed on me until I quit. Then I went back to work for Mr. Beloate. My Dad passed away during the time I worked at Beloate's Trim Shop. So, I didn't have my Dad or my mother, now. I was eighteen years old.

While I was working at Palmer Upholstery Shop I got a call. This guy called to offer me a job doing payroll. I took the job. My present boss gave me a hard time by saying, "James, you're leaving me in a tight spot." But, I wasn't. He'd just given me the job in the first place because he felt sorry for me. He should've felt blessed that I could move on.

[James working in his office at Goldring Hauling, Inc.]

[Johnny Goldring kidding around with James. They were best buddies on and off the job.]

So . . . the man who called me to work doing payroll was Mr. Pete Goldring. So I went to work for P.A. Goldring Hauling, Inc. I would drive back and forth to Ft. Worth, but one day the car kept dying on me. My aunt was going to follow me to work. I jumped in the car and took off, and she got behind and couldn't see me. I got to work and called her. She said, "Yeah, I'm here. You were dust. You were gone. I couldn't catch up."

That car kept trying to die on me on the way to work, but I was stubborn and kept it going enough to get me there. I had me a Triumph car. Oh, it was my baby. It had a rubber bumper all the way around it. I called it my Blue Goose.

One day I was going to work, and I started getting sleepy. I knew I was getting sleepy because I get off the road and hear the rough edge. I went up and incline. Now, you could turn that Triumph on a dime. And on that incline, it rolled over. My trunk flew open. Something hit me on the head and knocked me out. When the car rolled it landed on its wheels at 5:30 A.M. on the freeway.

[James working hard in his office at Goldring Hauling, Inc. with Mr. Pete Goldring, his boss, talking to Mrs. Joyce Goldring in the background. That's her purse on the table.]

So when I came to, I said, "Golly, no windshield." So, I drove to the office and called my boss man and told him what happened. He just told Joyce, his wife who worked with him in the office, that he was going down to help James dispatch some trucks. He didn't want to worry Mrs. Goldring. So, he came down and sent me to the hospital for my shoulder. My shoulder had landed on the pavement. It wasn't broken, just tore up some skin. The top of the Triumph was flat. If I had my seat belt on I would have been dead, but I didn't have it on. At the hospital the officers gave me two tickets, one for a negligent collision and the other for leaving the scene of an accident. So, I got two tickets, and I lost my car.

Six months later, I had me an Austin-Healy quarter-ton pickup. This time I had no warning whatsoever. No falling asleep, no feeling the road condition change. No warning. I went under an underpass, and that was the last thing I remember. I went down the road from there about three or four miles from the underpass, and I woke up. I always wake up in time to see the accident. There wasn't a car in my left-hand lane or in the right-hand lane. Just a bobtail truck in front. He stopped for a red light. I panicked.

[Mr. Pete Goldring with his pickup he drove for the business where James worked. Almost every picture of him standing has him in that slouched position. It must have been "cool" in the 1940's.]

I hit him. And I tell you what, that was the biggest rear-end I'd ever seen in my life. My leg went clear back in my back in to my hip. Well, that time I didn't leave the scene of an accident. They carried me away from there. I wanted to get rid of that old pickup, but I didn't want to get rid of it that way. I realized the Lord didn't get my attention the first time on the first accident.

He got my attention the second time. I said, "You can do whatever you want to with my life, Lord. It's yours. Do what you want to do. I know you got something for me to do, but I don't know what it is."

Life is a series of thousands of tiny miracles. Notice them.

I could tell you every turn we made going to that hospital. When we reached the hospital, they asked me who was my doctor. They said, "We've got three doctors'"

I didn't care what they were. I'd have taken a baby doctor. I wanted something done. I had about $500.00 insurance at the time. One of the three agreed to take my case. The accident happened at 4:30 a.m. I tried to get them to cut my pants off for the X-Ray. But, no, that wouldn't have been any fun. They pulled them off of me. They X-rayed me and put my leg up in a pulley.

My Aunt came in about this time, and I managed to squeak out, "I...I...I'm okay." My voice cracked with each syllable. Then they gave me a shot. And then they took my leg out.

I remember telling someone later, "Man, I thought I'd gone to Hell and back. The pain wasn't but for two or three-seconds, but oh, it was bad."

They asked if I wanted another painkiller, but after those few seconds that first one had kicked in, so I said, "No, it's okay now."

The doctor had already set it the way he wanted it, so the next morning they were going to do surgery and move me. They were going to move me to another bed.

The doctor said, "No. First give him enough meds to put him to sleep."

So they put me to sleep. So, I went through the surgery where they put a steel rod in my leg, and a steel ball in my hip. I was in there about nine days.

Newman Brothers came to see me on a Friday. Under the effect of the medications, it seemed to me they had the biggest heads in the world.

One other time, they gave me a baked potato that was rotten. I was afraid to say something. I thought they'd put another IV in me. But, I didn't have to. Suddenly, I threw up that potato. The nurse chewed the cafeteria lady out for bringing me a rotten potato.

Some days, I'd shave and cut myself, and the nurse would come to put a band-aide over it. I talked too much because she said, "You better watch it. I'll put tape over your mouth, too."

While I was in there I had what had to be an army nurse. Old woman. She gave me a bed bath. She got done with me, I was pink all over. So, when I got where I could walk with my crutches, the Doc said I should leave. Those nurses were tough, but good. They were a true blessing and took good care of me.

I returned in about nine days in pretty bad pain. He fussed at me because I'd been up on the crutches too much. My bone was grinding rather than knitting. He put me in bed for a whole month flat of my back. I was still working for the Goldring's. The Goldring's were real nice to me.

P.S. You're looking at a miracle right there, that Mrs. Goldring managed to get them all to dress up and act civilized in front of the camera!

My aunt went to pay my ticket while I was in the hospital. She told the judge, "That boy's not going to fight that ticket. He's in a hospital with a broken leg and hip."

So she went out to the clerk to pay the fine. The clerk wouldn't accept it. It wasn't enough money. So she returned to the judge. And he set a different price and she paid it.

After that month, I went to stay with my step-mother in Decatur. The Goldring's brought paperwork for me to do.

[This was the Goldring's about that time: Johnny Lloyd, Kathy Elaine, Tony (Anthony) Arden, Joyce Margarite (Smith) Goldring, and Phidias (Pete) Arden Goldring.]

Finally, I went back to work on my crutches. At about this time, my aunt died. And I couldn't drive from Decatur to Ft. Worth to work, so I went to a Truck Stop right by the Goldring's office, and I lived there.

So I kept working for the Goldring's. Me and Mr. Goldring's son, Johnny, became real good friends. Well, just like brothers. The whole family treated me like family. Johnny would come over and aggravate me like brothers do.

[This is Johnny. He was always grinning and laughing and pulling pranks. He's burying Jay, Kathy's first baby, in the sandbox.]

My step-brother took me out on a blind date. The first time they fixed me up with a gal. I don't know what her name was, but I called her "Rain-in-the-face" because she was so stuck up that if it rained, it would rain right in her face. Then I got another blind date. She was a nurse going to Nursing School. She knew what I looked like but I didn't have no idea what she looked like. My step brother and my sister-in-law took me over to her apartment. Judy went in and got her. A girl came out, but it wasn't my blind date, it was her sister. I didn't know this.

I told my brother, "Oh, she's fat."

"You better shut-up. She's gonna come out here and whip you."

She didn't, but then my blind date came out. Her name was Regina. At the end of the date I kissed her cheek. She gave me a go-to-hell look and doubled up her fist like she was gonna hit me, but didn't.

Every two or three months we'd go on a date, but I never tried to kiss her. I didn't want to get beat up. Finally, we started getting romantic and everything. We couldn't get too romantic because we were always double dating. I didn't have a car then.

On one of my dates, my boss's wife, Mrs. Goldring, took me and Regina to the fair and the rodeo. Their younger son, Tony, was there, and he rode with us. When we got there, I got out of the door and with my crutches started walking toward the entrance. Tony got out and went around and opened the door for Regina. I think maybe I was supposed to do that. Too late. She had to run to catch up with me. They had a funhouse where the wind blows up the girl's dresses. She didn't like it, but she went through it. I thought it was fun. Then they had a moving barrel we tried to walk through. I fell. She went on through, and had them cut the motor off and help me out. They also had a romantic canal ride. And a place where they guessed your weight. He couldn't guess her weight. She didn't weigh much, about 165, back then.

Nature's miracles
are found in
even the
simplest
of
things.

Chapter 2

Regina and I were at the Rodeo, and she won a Hula doll.
She gave it to me to hold. We went through the Love
Tunnel, and I lost that Hula doll in the Love Tunnel. I got
her home and got myself back to the service station where I
lived.

The next morning when I got to work, Mrs. Goldring
chewed me out up one side and down the other one about
how I treated Regina. Evidently, I was supposed to open
doors for her, close them afterwards, and not run ahead of
her. And, l'm pretty sure Mrs, Goldring said it'd be a miracle
if Regina even wanted to see me again after being treated
that way.

Regina had a roommate, Sandy. I had a friend I had in
high school named Johnny Daniels. So we would double
date. Regina did see me again, so I got that miracle Mrs.
Goldring thought I might not. Regina proved to be patient
and sweet to me. It was Valentine's Day. Johnny Daniels
went and bought Sandy a big, expensive box of candy. And
I bought a little old box of ninety-nine cent hard candy. The
candies said, "Love you," "Be mine," and all that stuff. And
Sandy held that over Regina's head all the time, that I was
so cheap, I wouldn't buy the big box of candy.

We went out several times. I'd call Regina often from the
office. And when I was on the phone, Johnny Goldring
would hang up the telephone. Then he'd take me out for a

cold drink, so she couldn't reach me if she called back. So after a while, I'd tell him, "She's at work now."

So, he'd take me back to the office, and then I'd call her again. Johnny was always mischievous like that. Whenever I had my little old car, him and David Wise and some of the other drivers, picked that car up and put it in the front door.

Johnny was just like his dad. His dad would tell me about stuff he did when he was younger. Him and Blackie, his friend. Blackie was a trucker that worked with the Goldring's, and Johnny was a chip off the old shoulder.

Me and Regina kept going out together. On one date, I remember, she put ice down the back of my shirt. But, I couldn't get ice down the back of her shirt, so I put ice down the front of her blouse. By that time, we were really in love.

She was going to go back to Arizona. And Johnny would say, "No, James, she's not going to go back to Arizona. Until you say the magic words, she's not going to go."

We went on dating. And after each date, Johnny would ask, "Well?"

I'd say, "Naw, I didn't have the nerve."

April rolled around, and I finally asked her to marry me. Johnny Daniels was there and his girlfriend, Sandy. So, I held something out to Regina.

She asked, "What is that?"

"A ring."

She didn't let me get away with just saying that; she made me ask her to marry her.

She said, "You've got to call my dad."

Her Dad was a thousand miles away in Arizona. Pretty safe distance. I remember I called him.

I said, "Hello, sir. I've heard a lot about you."

In a deep voice, he said, "I've heard a lot about you, sonny boy."

That shook me up, in fact, I was shaking all over. I just held out the phone to Regina and said, "Take it, take it."

She did. She talked to her dad. Johnny Daniels and all them were laughing at me. That next day I took her into work and told Johnny Goldring that I'd asked her to marry.

Johnny said, "You knucklehead! Now, she'll go back to Arizona, because she's already got you wrapped up."

She went back to Arizona for about three months. We wrote love letters to each other. I would call her once a week, but I'd write her every day. My family were all surprised. They didn't think I'd ever get married.

Finally the day came. I had a week off from work to go out to Phoenix to go get married. When I came out to Phoenix to get married, I rode the bus. I had money in the bank, and wrote out a check for my ticket.

When I got as far as El Paso, I was having a problem and for relief, I took a whole box of X-Lax. I didn't take one, I took the whole box. The closer we got to Phoenix, the sicker I got.

When I got to Phoenix, I was surprised because I'd not realized how green Phoenix was. Of course, I wasn't feeling too good, and so everything looked green. Regina picked me up at the bus station. She wanted me to talk to her dad. Now, I had met her mother before. We were like two peas in a pod. We got along real good, her mother and me. And so, Regina wanted me to go talk immediately to her dad who was in the front bedroom.

But her Mom said, "No, let James go lie down, Regina. He's sick."

So I went to down in the back bedroom, and my stomach was killing me. I guess, looking back, the fact that I survived the effects of an entire box of Ex-Lax was a miracle. Ohhhh, l was sooooo sick.

I'm whining out loud, too. "You don't want to get married. I'm dying. You don't want to get married to me." Might have also been a miracle that my future father-in-law didn't kill me when he heard that.

Regina's sister slept in the third bedroom, and Regina's Dad made Regina sleep on the couch. He said, "You might get my oldest daughter (Regina's sister), but you ain't getting my youngest daughter." I think if I was marrying the oldest one, he'd have been jumping up and down with joy. Considering how I felt, he didn't have any worries any way.

So Regina and I finally went to get our blood work. I had to go to the office which was full of people. Every time they tried to take my blood, I'd excuse myself, go outside, and throw up. I did that twice before they got my blood. Between the Ex-Lax experience and the blood work, the Phoenix trip was not going really well. Then we went back over to Regina's home.

We had to go before the Justice of the Peace to get the marriage license. And then we went to the park. Ah, now, I could finally relax a little.

Nope. The car broke down. Here came a guy on a motorcycle, an auto mechanic, but he couldn't get it started. Then a guy in a jeep arrived. He couldn't get it fixed, either.

So the jeep driver said, "I'll take one of you all to a phone so you can call your mother."

So, we let my sister-in-law, Joan go. He floor-boarded it, and the front end went off the ground! This was the first time Regina and I had been alone, alone.

All by ourselves. It was there at the Hole-In-The-Rock by the Zoo. Regina said,

"Did you know that true love got killed out here?"

"No." It didn't bother me any. But, we walked around, and I saw all these holes in the ground. "Those are snake holes!"

If I'd seen a snake, I would've headed back to Texas immediately!

Then about nine or ten o'clock at night, I was drinking water from a water fountain. And that water was hot! We finally got home. Then we went to Legend City. We were going to ride on a Sky Ride.

I asked, "Will this hold us all?"

The operator of the Sky Ride said, "Yes."

He locked us in. We decided we didn't want to ride if we had to be locked in. So we didn't have that adventure. I didn't test my guardian angel that day.

When we got married, I couldn't have asked for a better father-in-law. His name was James Thomas Warren Smith. She had a brother-in-law and a sister-in-law. One's birthday was November 11th and one was November 9th. Mine fell between them on the tenth. Regina Lee had the same "RL" initials as my mother and step-mother. Rosa Lucinda was my mother's name. My step-mother's name was Ruby Lee.

I always said, "If God had not picked out my women for me, I would have been in trouble."

We got married, and we didn't tell nobody that we didn't have no money to go back to Texas. Regina's family gave us twenty dollars. And I had twenty with me. Although I had money in the bank in Texas, they wouldn't take a personal check out there in Arizona for anything.

So . . . we had fifteen cents left between us now. I saved a dime to call my boss, Mr. Goldring, when I got back to Texas. So we had a five-cent pack of gum for twenty-six hours on that bus. At each stop, we'd get off and walk around, because we didn't want anyone to know we didn't have no money. So, for twenty-six hours we lived on love.

When we got to Ft. Worth, I called my boss man about what was going on. Then we got a cab, and I paid with a check. Then we got a big ol' Texas steak. I kept yakking, and she couldn't eat hers because she got so tickled at me.

Then me and my boss man, Mr. Goldring, we picked out a car. It was a lemon, but we picked it out. Then we got in the car and Regina and I spent the night at my mother's house. Then we got us a garage apartment.

Mrs. Goldring threw a wedding shower for us in their front yard at 8550 Meadowbrook Drive in Ft. Worth.

Gee

Golly—

A SHOWER!
for
JAMES & REGINA
ROBERTS

SUNDAY JULY 10
3 P.M. - 5 P.M.

8550 MEADOWBROOK

[Kathy even did a cute little invitation that was mailed out to everyone.]

We had the shower under the trees in the beautiful front yard on Meadowbrook. She loved her "adopted" brother James, and she thought Regina was beautiful and sweet. We got a lot of nice deals and gifts. Kathy Goldring and Claudia Bennett helped set pretty tables up and served punch and cake.

That night Johnny Goldring came over. I went to the door, and yelled back at Regina, "Johnny's here."

"Well, invite him in."

"I can't. He's gone."

So Regina and I ate breakfast about seven, looked outside, and toilet paper was hanging all over the trees.

I went over and called my step-sister, thinking they had done it for our shower night, but she said, "No, it wasn't Jimmy."

So I called my boss man. Mr. Goldring said, "Johnny just got in. Don't worry about it, James. Johnny'll be over after while."

I said, "Okay."

Johnny was lucky that night, because usually the cops patrol that neighborhood real well.

Pretty soon, Johnny shows up at the house. He didn't know Regina very well, and Regina didn't know him that well. She just knew that he was mischievous. She puts her hair in rollers and gets the frying pan.

When Johnny comes, I tell him, "I'll help you out." I turn to Regina and say, "Hit him, Baby, hit him!" Ha!

She reared back like she was going to hit him. Johnny owned up to having toilet-papered the place.

He walked toward his red Mustang. "I'll go get a buddy to help me."

She followed right behind him, brandishing that skillet. "No, you won't." She acted like she was going to bust his windshield out!

He said, "Okay. I'll wash it all down."

"No, you won't."

She made him pick all that toilet paper out of the trees and put it in a trash bag. He had to use fishing poles to get all of it down. We had toilet paper for a whole three months. We didn't have to buy any toilet paper!

Afterwards, we asked how he managed not to get caught doing it. He grinned. "Aww, we know all the cops. I just waved as they went by."

Regina and I had been married for three months, and I took her out to the Farmer's Daughter and we had a romantic meal. And then sometime afterwards, me and Johnny went out somewhere and Sandy and Regina went out. We'd all agreed to be in at a decent hour around nine or ten o'clock. Right. Well, the plan was good, but it didn't quite turn out that way. So here come Johnny and me home about two o'clock in the morning. And we had gone to a striptease joint. I don't smoke. Period. So Regina could smell that smoke on my clothes. So I told her that Johnny twisted my arm and made me go to that striptease joint. She didn't buy that.

The next morning Johnny asked, "James, did I get

you in trouble? Did I get you in trouble?" He was laughing and grinning, hoping he had gotten me in trouble.

I said, "No."

Disappointed, he said, "Darn it."

He was always that way, playing little jokes. One time he came over to see me about two o'clock in the morning. He'd been out, running around putting shaving cream in Donald's (Don Lee) his half-brother's truck in the seat where he wouldn't see it, would scoot in and sit in it. Then he came over to my place and tried to put shaving cream on me!

There was an Arab guy who had a truck that worked for Johnny's dad, Mr. Goldring, once in a while. And Johnny put a pig in that truck! The Arab had a fit. He had to clean that pig stuff out of his truck. Johnny was always doing something like that.

He had boards with nails in them set out, and he'd zoom by the cops, making them follow him, and they'd run over all those nails. I figure now, that Johnny had a pretty busy guardian angel on his shoulder, too.

He took after his Dad, Mr. Goldring. Mr. Goldring told me when he was a kid, he'd lock the screen door, lock his mother out of the house, and jump up and down, make faces and stick out his tongue. Whew, she was mad!

One time Pete Goldring knocked the horn off of a cow. He told his parents that the cow was shedding. He told me once about an incident with Blackie, longtime trucker friend, who was scared of everything. Mr. Goldring yelled out, scared Blackie, who jumped up and ran over a board and got a nail in his foot. That wasn't intended to happen.

He just meant to scare Blackie. So Johnny sort of took after his dad in the mischievous department.

[This is Mr. Pete Goldring on the family horse, Bambi. Behind him is Tony. Family friends could bring babies. Bambi was so gentle, he would only walk slowly when a baby was on board.]

The first eighteen months that me and Regina were married, I was King of the Hill. Every time I'd say something, Regina would jump to get whatever I wanted. Then when my oldest daughter, Ora Licinda, was born, that King title went out the door so fast I couldn't believe it! I woke up, snapped my fingers and nothing happened. But, Regina snapped hers, and I jumped! I would be the one jumping ever since.

My first daughter, Ora Licinda Roberts was born. She was truly a miracle many times over in my life, and still is.

My half-sister, Lily, when she was born, she was my dad's pride and joy. When she was about two years old, he was singing a song to his boss about "how drunk I do feel." After my dad died, it hit Lily hard. Me and Lily's brother, David, would get anything she wanted if we could. One time Lily had a boyfriend she was serious about, and my step-mother wanted me to have a talk with her. I did.

a daughter
is a miracle that
never ceases to
be miraculous.

She said, "I want to get married, James, I want to get married." But I kept talking to her. The next day he went into the army, and she called me and chewed me out.

Once with Regina, Lily had cut her hair, then went around trying to find a beauty shop to fix the mess she'd made. Lily needed a guardian angel that day.

Regina's and I had a first Christmas together. Regina was very artistic. She had a tumbleweed. It had nests and birds on it. When she became pregnant with Ora, Mr. and Mrs. Goldring wouldn't let me take her to the hospital. They said, "You call us. No way are you going to drive her over there as nervous as you'll be." On January 18th, we'd been married for eighteen months, less about ten days, and Ora was born.

The Goldring's came and got Regina and me in the Cadillac. Regina was in labor for twenty-six hours. She had small bones and no matter how tiny, the baby would not come out. So it was going to be a C-section birth. I remember holding her hand.

She wanted her mama, but her mother was in Arizona. Green stuff started coming out of Regina's mouth, and I started crying. I went out of the room and bawled.

The doctors did do a Caesarian on her. She weighed 230 pounds. She had pneumonia, because they had not kept her lung pump clear. She busted open. She had gotten up and then stumbled back to bed. The doctor was bug-eyed and shocked, and that scared her.

And we got a special miracle for Regina that day. The pneumonia was got under control, and finally, Ora was born. I thought they were being real mean to her. They had her by her feet and treating her like a dishrag. It made me upset. Of course, they were just clearing her lungs and making sure she would cry. But, I was still upset. I didn't want anyone hurting that baby.

I counted my blessings that day, since Regina and the baby were okay. We brought her home in our old Chevrolet. She went there to be born in a Cadillac and came home in a Chevy. We stayed with my step brother and his wife for a couple of days. Then we all came home, and that started the sleepless nights.

One day I was going to work, I went to sleep and drove about a mile, stopped and got me something to drink and went on to work. I've had sleep apnea all my life. But, it was worse with the sleepless nights.

Always believe that something wonderful is about to happen.

When I used to go to sleep in class, one teacher would pop me on my ear to wake me up. Then I had another one, Mr. Hagman, that would cover my head up and let me sleep in class. He was my favorite teacher. He would tell funny stories about his house and what-not. He was the only one that ever gave me a whipping. He was dating the lady PE teacher. We had a donkey basketball game. Me and Tim and one other boy didn't want to go. If we all went, he'd get to go, but we three didn't want to. We were in the library. Mr. Hagman came in and told us to be quiet. We weren't. He took us all three to the office and used the paddle on us. He was a big man. It didn't hurt badly, but it stung. He's the one that failed me in seventh grade, but he was still my favorite teacher. I had him in ninth grade, too.

I also failed music-chorus in the seventh grade. I failed English, Texas history and the music class. The English teacher offered to let me transfer to another teacher if I wanted to, but I was afraid of any change, so went ahead and took her. But the next year, she wasn't that bad. Women weren't that bad, really, if I gave them a fair chance. I had a lot of life lessons to teach me that.

[James as a young cowboy on a bucking bronco. Photo shared by his daughters.]

I had gotten that bad attitude against women due to my dad's attitude toward my mom. He was the boss in everything. But, my step-mom wanted equal say, and she eventually did get equal say. My dad did not claim to be a great role-model.

He'd say, "Do what I tell you, and we'll be fine. Do as I say, not as I do."

He wanted me to do office work. When it came time to do paperwork and what-not, he wanted me to do it.

Anyhow, the sleep apnea continued into my grown years, and affected me on the way to work with Mr. Goldring, right after our daughter, Ora, came home. My sister-in-law came to live with us then. She tried to live on her own, but she just couldn't do it.

She was the type of woman who loved me as her brother-in-law, but she wanted to be boss. But, she also didn't want anyone else running over me, just her.

My oldest sister and I drifted apart. It wasn't her fault. It was mine. She had her version of how she treated mom and dad, and I had my version. She did everything in her power to be a good sister, but I did everything in my power not to be a good brother to her. So, we had years and years and years when we didn't communicate. She tried to, but I didn't. I still had some life lessons to learn.

Going on with the miracle of Ora. When she was little we took her to a restaurant one time. She'd start bawling. Every time we'd say stop, she'd hush. But every time we went in a restaurant, she'd throw a fit, and we'd have to leave.

We had a crib for Ora that her uncle Albert made for his kids and passed it on for her. But, all of a sudden, she didn't want to sleep in it, and she'd cry. I'd get up with her and hold her and she quiet, but when I'd put her back down, she'd cry. I finally gave her a whipping. That didn't work, either. I put her in bed with us and she slept just fine.

When Ora started walking, she was really a pain. She'd do a whole bunch of things. One time Ora messed her pants. Joan was asleep. Ora had gotten her hand in her diaper, and was going to feed Joan. We walked in just in time to save Joan from getting a mouthful of poop.

Ora was always running off. One time me and Joan were at home and watching Ora. She crawled out of the house and went over to a neighbor's house. We went hunting for her. The neighbor's had heard what they thought was a cat messing around in the yard. They investigated and saw Ora go out to the road, so Joan and I went out to get her. I was so scared and so mad, I never even told that guy thank you for letting us know where she was. She got a good spanking for that prank.

Another time my wife, Regina, and I were at work, and it grew quiet, which was unusual since we'd just gotten a puppy. Ora'd make noise with that puppy, but Regina didn't hear anything. She wondered where Ora was. That time Regina found her at the neighbor's back of us. She had the puppy with her. The folks had a hole in the screen door, and she just went in the house. She'd climbed up in a playpen and then couldn't get out. The hole was big enough for her, but not for her mother, so Regina had to break into the house to get Ora out and take her home.

One time she got into the medicine cabinet, and took a bunch of stuff. She went kind of crazy and dry-mouthed. But Regina called the doctor, gave her some Valium, calmed her down, and she was okay after all of that wore off.

Once we were out in the yard working and planting some tulips. And boom-that kid was gone out of sight before we knew it. My sister-in-law, Joan, had just gotten home from work and put on her MuMu to go to bed, but she jumped in the car to help hunt. She found Ora on the freeway just walking down beside the freeway. Joan ran down the embankment to get her. Of course, her MuMu was flying around. She got Ora, brought her back home, but Joan was shaking all over, it scared her so badly..

One time I talked to my step-mother on the phone in one room. Meanwhile, in the kitchen, Ora climbed up on the counter, and she was throwing eggs on the floor. Oh, boy. I didn't whip her, but I grabbed her and put her in her little high chair.

I said, "I just dare you to get down. I double-dog dare you."

She decided it wouldn't be wise to get up with daddy in that mood. She stayed put.

One time she was taking dance lessons (ballet or tap) and put on her pretty costume, but she hadn't put her panties on. Regina was so embarrassed, but it didn't seem to bother Ora. She danced away happy and free, in many ways.

Joan and her mother took her to the eye doctor once. My wife had taught her the vowels like a-e-i-o-u. The doctor came out after the examination and asked my wife, "Is Ora mentally challenged? I pointed to the letters and she just grunts."

So Regina went in with the doctor. "Ora, pronounce the letter as the doctor points to them, don't grunt."

Ora said, "Okay. A-E-I-O-U" as clear as could be after her Mama told her to.

One time I went home and made a roast for her when she came home. She had stayed over and talked and talked at her girlfriend's house, but she apologized for being late. Needless to say, we had a well-done roast.

We had a dog named George. George had started out as a neighborhood dog who would bring things over into our yard. We lived in our first apartment about a month, and then moved to a house. We stayed there about two years or so. We had our first Christmas in that home.

Ora was about three years old. We stopped at A&W and got two coke floats. We got Ora a small one. She got mad at that and dumped it in my lap. Her mother told her she was going to get a whipping, but she didn't get one.

Ora said, "I'm mad now, but I'll apologize tomorrow."

She did say, "I'm sorry, Daddy," the next day, so she kept her word.

One day I went to pick up Ora at high school. I saw some boys jump the fence. I said if they can jump the fence, so can I. And I did jump. I got caught in the middle of the fence. Some of the boys knew Ora.

They said, "Mr. Roberts, we'll help you down."

I said, "No, I'll get down." I did, but I tore my pants, and Regina had to fix them. I learned I wasn't young anymore.

Then we bought a house closer to work. We lost that house in Texas. I couldn't make payments for a while on it, and I wouldn't sell it, so they repossessed it. Somebody took over the payments.

Johnny came over and we went to the wrestling matches, and Regina had told her people at work that she was going to introduce me to them. Joan babysat until Regina had to go to work, and she'd drop her off at the nursing home where Regina worked. And they asked, "Ain't you worried about your husband?"

She said, "No, I ain't worried about James."

So off we went to the wrestling matches. Now, at that time I didn't know that Johnny drank any kind of liquor. But, he did, on occasion. So, we each had a beer apiece. Then suddenly it turned into five or six beers each. And I could tell those wrestlers weren't hitting each other. They were missing each other by a country mile. At least, from my side of drinking a half-dozen beers, it seemed that way.

So Johnny said, "Okay, James. Let's go."

Johnny drove. "If I can't drive, I'll call Mom and Dad."

And when we got home, I said I was going to pick up Regina from work, but Johnny said, "No, you're not. You're in no condition to drive."

So he took me to the nursing home. And he told me, "James, don't get out of the car. She won't be able to tell you've been drinking if you just stay in the car."

Hey, you don't tell a drunk to do something. Not this drunk, anyway. I got out of that car. Nothing was right. The sidewalk shifted funny. I couldn't seem to stand up straight. Regina saw me, and her eyes opened wide. She and Ora flew out that door. She didn't tell those people she worked with goodbye or kiss my foot. She made a bee-line for me. I managed to stumble back into the car. Even I noticed that car smelled like a brewery. I mean it stunk.

Johnny said, "I'll take you all out to dinner and get you something to eat."

He did. At the restaurant I had to go the bathroom. He wouldn't say anything to Regina. He just sat there and grinned at her. It did not help her disposition. She did not smile back at him.

Finally, we got home. Some of the effects of those beers had worn off what with eating and everything. So now, I could tell Regina was mad.

Inside the house, I told her, "Get me a glass of water."

She said, "Okay."

But she must have forgot the water. She came back with a glass of rum. Humph. I don't like rum. She knew I didn't like rum. But, that time . . . well, I looked into her eyes, and I drank it. I knew I was in trouble.

When Johnny got home he was happy. Mrs. Goldring asked what was going on.

Johnny said, "I got James in trouble again. I got James in trouble." He grinned.

He was right. I got the silent treatment for about three days. But, finally Regina figured I'd learned my lesson, and she spoke to me.

Another thing Johnny did one time was when they had a Chow-chow dog named Yaqui. He picked that Chow up and threw him in a mud puddle. Yaqui turned around and bit Johnny in the butt. He ran in the house and poured alcohol on his rear, and he was groaning.

[Yaqui]

His mother asked, "What's the matter?"

Johnny said, "Ohhh, ahhh nothing." He never threw that doggie in the mud puddle again. Guess Johnny had a few life lessons to learn, too.

His dilemma reminded me that when I was younger my aunt had a Chow-chow dog, Bear. She was a little bitty woman. I saw my aunt pull on that dog, pick him up by the tail and throw him in the trailer and what-not. Her being so small, I figured I could do anything she could do. So I sat down and pulled his tail. He growled at me. I pulled it a little bit harder, and he growled again. Third time, he forgot to growl.

Bear sat on top of me! He slapped me with his paw and shut one of my eyes. My aunt came out, grabbed the dog and threw him in the trailer. I went on to school, and was sent to the nurse with my injured eye. When the school nurse asked what happened, I said, "I pulled the dog's tail, and he hit me."

The nurse got real mad and came out to the house. She wanted that dog tied up, claiming it was mad because it had attacked a child.

My aunt said, "No, I'm not tying that dog up. If you'd had an idiot out here pulling your tail, you might attack, too." My aunt had down-home, common sense.

So from that point, I learned to pat Bear, but I left his tail alone. Sometimes miracles come in small lessons, a lot of them from the animal world if we'll just pay attention.

Bear never would kill a chicken, but he'd put his paw on it, and pluck out one feather at a time. Of course, that chicken was squawking like crazy. So my uncle decided he was going to break Bear of that habit. So he hits the poor dog across the back with a two-by-four. Bear turned around and growled and snarled at him. My uncle threw that two by four down and went in the house.

One day my aunt was living in a trailer in my brother-in-law's yard. And my aunt was sitting and resting and told her brother-in-law to go out and get her pack of cigarettes.

So, in he went to get those cigarettes and Bear grabbed his hand. It didn't bite him, but he dropped the smokes.

He went back to my aunt and told her, "If you want those damned cigarettes, you can go get them yourself."

The water man came to the front door, went inside to get the water jug, and Bear never bothered him. They had a bulldog named Skipper, and that bulldog was always jumping on Bear. Bear was really gentle with him, but my uncle got tired of it and separated the two dogs. He patted on Bear's tail, and Bear thought it was the bulldog.

My uncle said, "Get him, Bear!"

And Bear got that dog, shook him, hit his head against a rock. For a full month there that bulldog would be around the yard, but he wouldn't have nothing to do with Bear. Then he'd get brave enough to have another go. Bear would give him another whipping, and the bulldog would act like he was dying. Uncle would separate them over and over.

One time when I was about seven or eight, I played with my aunt's goldfish. Those goldfish started to die, one by one. My aunt kept wondering what was happening to her fish. I didn't tell her that I'd taken them out of the water to play with them. I didn't know at the time that would hurt them. I was just playing with the squirmy things.

I'm sure I tried the patience of my aunt because I was a curious boy, and wanted to know how things worked. And I didn't feel, since she was just a woman, that I needed to bother her with questions I figured she wouldn't know the answers to, anyhow.

One time I had cut my eyebrow somehow, and I'd hidden under the bed. She got home and called me out from under the bed. I guess I was a mischievous little boy.

Years later, when Mr. and Mrs. Goldring sold the business out, I wanted to leave. My wife didn't. That was entirely me. I wanted to get away from my older sister. When we'd made the contract, there was a clause in it, that if he sold, I got to stay on, and I did. I wanted to come to Arizona. So, Mr. and Mrs. Goldring brought me to Arizona.

I could always read Mr.Goldring's mind before he ever said anything. I knew usually what he was thinking. One episode was that they had a bookkeeper. His name was Clyde. So l was doing the payroll.

Clyde came in and told me, "James, tell you what. I'll help you do the payroll tomorrow."

Well, when tomorrow got here, he didn't help me. Then I'd be doing it Saturday morning when the men came in to get their paychecks. Mr. Goldring was asking about the late payroll.

I said, "He was supposed to help. He's invisible. I can't see him, anyway."

Clyde later asked, "James, why'd you tell Mr. Goldring that I was invisible? I wasn't here?"

"Well, you wasn't," I answered. Eventually, Mr. Goldring found out that Clyde was stealing money from the company, Goldring Hauling, Inc. Clyde went to prison.

All the Goldring's treated me like I was one of the family. All of them did. Me and Johnny was real close. One day when it was muddy, I used Kathy's car, a 1964 baby blue Ford Galaxy 500. That meant only 500 of them were made. Kind of special car, but the Goldring's once and awhile let me use the cars when needed. This day it was her car. I didn't want to walk through those truck yards, so used her car, and scratched the car up. When I got back from picking up the tickets, I told Mr. Goldring what happened and showed him the dent. He didn't get mad, but he didn't let me drive that car anymore, either. Kathy never had said anything about it to me, so I guess she didn't get upset by it, neither.

Kathy's 1964 Blue Ford Galaxy was solid, not a white top. She still has it on blocks in her back yard. The only scratches on it, were those I got on it in the mud that day, and one Tony got on it when he backed into the barbed wire fence at home. They are very tiny. She did not get mad at either of them. She drove it through college and through ten years of marriage and kids. She named it "Baby Blue".

One time, me and my wife Regina, Johnny and David Wise and another driver went to East Texas to pick up some trucks. The car wouldn't hardly run, but we made it up there. People that were hitchhiking would see us and put their thumb down, not up! We got up there, got the diesel trucks, Johnny and the others drove them, and Regina and I drove the car back. We actually got that old clunker back home! Now, there was a miracle!

As I said before, I had sleep apnea, and I'd be doing payroll and go to sleep.

Johnny would come in and see me and say, "James, how do you do it? You're sound asleep and writing."

Luckily, when I woke up, I could always locate any errors that I'd made. Johnny and I did lots of things together. He and I were really close and pulled pranks on each other all

the time. And pranks on others, too. But . . . whenever Johnny got married, I came out to San Angelo to see him.

[This is Johnny sitting with his niece, Hollyanna, out at the cottage where the Goldring's lived beside their daughter, Kathy. All the kids loved Johnny.]

He didn't laugh much, not much kidding and fun was left in him. Years later in his fifties, he died of cancer.
He wasn't the same Johnny I knew. He was tamed, and didn't seem too happy.

Before he passed, Pete and Joyce Goldring moved to Buffalo Springs, out in East Texas. I went to visit them there and helped Mr. Goldring feed the cows and mow the yard and such, and got plenty dirty and dusty. He always considered me as one of his sons. We laughed a lot.

Me and Kathy got to know each other better in later years. After Johnny died, I tried to be a brother to her. Mrs. Goldring passed away, too. Kathy took care of her mother at home until the day she passed. I came out to visit Kathy and Mr. Goldring, her Dad. I helped him build a small brick porch for Kathy's back side yard so she wouldn't have to step into the mud to take her trash out and stuff. I also got to meet some of Kathy's writer friends, the McKee's, Shirley and Mac. They took to me like family just as Kathy did. We had a good time together.

She took good care of her Dad. Kathy had two children, Jay Hamilton Shaffer and Hollyanna Margarite Shaffer. She had a rough marriage and got divorced, and took back her maiden name of Goldring. Her ex was a control freak and stalker for years after the divorce, but she persevered. She took care of both her parents for about the last fifteen years of their lives. She, too, said there was a great difference in her brother, Johnny, after his marriage. She loved both her brothers, and she really missed Johnny after his passing, and missed Tony because he never came around after Johnny and Mr. and Mrs. Goldring passed away.

Anyhow, back to when Mr. Goldring took me to Arizona. He took me to visit lots of places on the way, and finally took me to my mother-in-law's. I stayed with my mother-in-law until I got a job. My wife was back in Texas, keeping up the house, working, taking care of the baby and her sister, Joan. After three months, I got the job at Paloma Ranch doing pay roll. Back home, I knew it was rough on Regina, and she didn't want to come out to Arizona, but she finally did. I went back to Texas to get Regina, Ora and Aunt Joan. I will never ask another woman to give up her career, and I'd want her to be close to her parents. Regina didn't want to come to Arizona, but she did for me.

At one time while we were apart, Ora told a nurse's aide that I had been killed by Indians. Regina had to tell them that I was alive in Arizona and Ora was watching too many westerns on TV.

When I was first offered the job at Paloma Ranch in 1970-71, my mother-in-law took me out there the first time.

We thought we'd gotten lost. It was about eighty miles out. They liked me in the interview. They were interviewing another guy. He didn't have children, but I did. So they wanted a family man, so they gave me a job on March 13th.

I had an International pickup. We looked like the Beverly Hillbillies with it loaded down and my sister-in-law came with us, and she had her Pinto loaded, too. We drove straight through with short hour stops now and again. Then the ranch furnished us a van to move us out, too. We got there and lived on Staff Row, they called it. It was a real nice house with a big fence in the back. Bob, the collie, would always jump over that fence, though. He would attack dogs, but wait until their backs were turned. Even so, he never won a dog fight. Don't think he would even if it was a Chihuahua.

There was a neighbor who had a bulldog puppy named Max. We kept telling him, "Watch out. That pup's going to get grown one of these days."

Sure enough, it did, got hold of Bob and wouldn't let him go. We hit them with the water-hose. I hollered, "Bob, get in the house." He did. Quickly.

We had to take him to the vet and get him stitched up.

The neighbor lady would spray a lot of perfume on her clothes before hanging them out on the line to dry. Bob would go pull them down and make love-hump-on them. He'd pull them over to our house.

Sometimes I was pretty mean to that dog, but he behaved pretty well for me. He minded me better than the kids did. Overall, he was a good dog. I think his problems came from being really mistreated before we had him. In later years, he just wandered off one day and died.

The supervisor would run by every morning, and Bob would jump the fence and chase him. Then he'd come back to the house, wanting me to let him in the back yard. I did for a while, but got tired of that. So, one time I threw him over the fence. That tore his hip out of place. I tied him up to keep him in. I'd leave, and Regina would untie him so he could get in the shade. It was awful hot out there. We stayed at that house about three or four months.

They built new houses, and we were the first ones to get one of those new ones. That was a special blessing to have a new home. We lived there until I quit years later.

When Regina finally came out to Arizona, she wanted a nursing job, but there wasn't one where we lived. So, she became a substitute teacher, and she cleaned the big house. She enjoyed her arts and crafts.

My oldest daughter, Ora, went to school there at Paloma. One day I got a call that Ora wasn't reading. Regina went to investigate. Ora had her book in her desk, but she wouldn't get it out. Regina made her get it out. Then Regina saw the teacher shaking the book in Ora's face and screaming at her. Regina then chewed out the teacher. So, we set up a parent teacher meeting, and Regina went. The principal had to be in there with them to keep them from verbally fighting. There was another incident where Ora had done her homework and done more that she was told. The teacher called and told Regina she didn't have to do all that. She needed to follow directions. So Regina and the teacher got into it again.

Ora was real little, and the others picked on her, especially one boy. The teacher did nothing about it. One night Regina and I went hunting for a garden area. It was not quite sundown. We had an International pickup. I knew it couldn't get bogged down or stuck anywhere. It was safe to roam around all over the ranch in it. Now, Regina had been raised in this area, and she knew about the cotton fields and the run-offs and such. We got in an "iffy" area, and she told me to immediately back it out.

"We're going to bog down. Back up."
I didn't pay any attention to her. She was a woman, and didn't know about things like International pickups. I made it around a corner, but all four tires and wheels got bogged down. Way down. So, another lesson learned. Guess she did know what she was talking about. And, I was worried being way out there on the ranch land. This would have been a good time for my over-worked guardian angel to show up.

He performs wonders that cannot be fathomed, miracles that cannot be counted.

Job 5:9

Now, it was late in the evening and the coyotes were howling. I took my boots off, stepped off into the mud. Of course, my feet were covered in seconds. Then I couldn't get my boots back on because of the thick mud. So I went walking up to the national camp. That's the camp where the field hands stayed. They spoke only Spanish, and I couldn't make them understand me. One ditch rider recognized me as the man who made out the payroll, and he could speak English, so he tied the company pickup to my truck. He was the blessing of this adventure. Or, at least, I thought he was. But, poor guy. Instead of pulling me out, he pulled the bumper off the pickup.

Then he saw the tractor out in the field. "I'll go out and get the tractor and bring it back."

Then he got the tractor stuck in the cotton field. I'll give him all the credit for saving us, though. He didn't give up. He radioed in to the other ditch rider. They had an old troubleshooting pickup they used to carry things on to do repairs and grease the pumps and such. So Regina and I climbed into the back of that dirty pickup and they carry us home. She was not happy about that greasy, dirty pickup.

The next morning I told the boss what happened. First, he went and chewed off that guy for pulling off the company bumper. They had to get Caterpillars to get the tractor out, hooked it up to my International and pulled it out. He took my pickup back to the shop and steam cleaned it for me. Come to find out, we were just on this side of the canal from where the garden was. So, we got mighty close.

I was elected to be on the school board. It was a tie vote 13 to 13. And my opponent's daughter drew my name from the jar. So I had the position for four years. After four years I ran again and won. The first seven years were okay. I enjoyed it. The eighth year was terrible. There were many people to deal with that weren't pleasant and many hard decisions I had to make.

But even among the terrible things that happened, one wonderful miracle happened. In 1974 we had a daughter born on May 9th, Joanna Lee (Lee Lee) Roberts.

I'm Just Sayin' Signs

She was determined to be born that day. We knew it would have to be a C-section. In February we had gone to the doctor when Regina got pregnant. The first assistant did a rabbit test on her and then sent her in to the doctor, but the doctor didn't believe Regina was pregnant.

Dr. Saide said, "That ain't nothing but dang ordinary every-day fat." Crying, Regina left the office. She knew better because she could feel the baby moving.

The next Monday we were called back in for the results of the rabbit test, and the doctor had to apologize. So on May 9th, 1974, Lee Lee was born. The specialist who was supposed to be there for the delivery was flying and making a night landing too late. So Dr. Saide had to deliver her.

The doctor came in the next morning and asked, "How's it going?"

We said, "Fine."

And I said, "Did you tie the tubes? You better have." The one that was supposed to have done the C-section looked at the chart.

"Yeah, we tied them."

Ora had been praying for a baby sister. And I had gone around making bets that it would be a boy, so I was a welsher on a lot of "boy" bets. But, I wasn't too disappointed. I had two wonderful daughters.

So by the time I'd served seven years and had started on my eighth year on the school board, my youngest daughter, Lee Lee was going to school. She had a learning disorder. She couldn't be still and such. It wasn't disrespect or behavior problem, but a medical problem. The teacher said her lifespan wasn't that long, and she put her in a box. Regina went down and talked to the principal. So they got her special tested. The other board member suggested she be evaluated for other learning problems. The principal didn't want to do that, but the other board members told her to. So she was evaluated and put in special classes. At that time those weren't available in Paloma, so she went to Gila Bend. When they got a special education teacher at Paloma, Lee Lee went back to Paloma.

[*Joanna Lee (Lee Lee) - 4 years old, Ora Licinda - 10 years old, Regina Lea - 32 years old, James Fred - 37 years . A Beautiful family!*]

I got to give my oldest daughter, Ora, her eighth-grade diploma, since I was on the board at the time. They graduating class went to the Grand Canyon, the teacher, Mrs. Johnson, five girls and one boy. They had quite a trip. They tied the boy up one day. Mr. Stant was a teacher and

Hawaiian. He taught both my daughters the Hawaiian dances. He talked Ora into going down the Grand Canyon, and on the way back, she had to talk him into making it.

She'd say, "You can make it. You can make it."

They went to the slide rock. She did okay, but she tore her pants. She enjoyed the trip a lot.

That eighth year I was on the board, we were trying to get rid of the principal and the third grade teacher. It was her first year, and the principal was supposed to be guiding her. And neither was doing their job. We had a school board meeting one night that lasted until midnight. We didn't get rid of either one of them.

Poor Regina had a reputation that she didn't deserve. She was the boss and controlled everything and had a temper, and I didn't-so everyone thought. That was wrong. She always backed me up in public. If she disagreed, she'd wait until we got home. Then she'd let me know what was what. But in public, even if I was wrong, she'd back me up. I always appreciated that.

Some of the things I've done in life, I wouldn't have done if it hadn't have been for her. I would never have been on the school board or joined the Lion's Club or the PTA.

The year Lee Lee was in the first grade, Regina made a special costume for me and dared me to wear it. When the kids saw it, they didn't know what to think about that six-foot bunny. When the general manager came in at work, he was a little shocked, too. The bunny went to the school. The class played musical chairs. And it was down to one little boy and me-the bunny. He got to the seat first, but I knocked him out of it. The Easter Bunny had to win! But, my daughter Lee Lee was crying because the other kids were telling her that was her daddy.

She said, "No. That was the real Easter Bunny."

When she got home, Regina had to get out the costume and explain that it was "her daddy" in the costume. She was okay with it then.

[This is a good photo of the Smith and Roberts family.]

I wore the Easter Bunny for over twenty years. For the first few years, my wife would make all the eggs and the baskets, but when it got too big, we got the Lion's Club involved, so I was their Easter Bunny, too. The PTA was also involved. Everyone enjoyed the Easter Bunny. One year I was the PTA leader. I learned that sometimes the only way you could get people to come to the school board meetings was to make them mad. To get them to a PTA meeting was simple: I put a reminder in their pay check in such a way that they thought it was from the General Manager, and so everyone showed up.

For Halloween, Regina always made a costume, too. She would stay at the house for those that came to trick or treat. She'd dress up like a witch and hand out candy. Sometimes I was a lion, sometimes The Great Pumpkin,

and Hawaiian Royal, and all different things. Everyone enjoyed it. We had hayrides that the company offered. They'd have a decorating party. Whatever house was best decorated would win a prize-- $10.00, $15.00, and $25.00. Regina always loved to decorate, and I had to help her.

At Christmas I'd put up signs in the yard, and she had a cart that she filled with a manger scene. Had the camel and all that.

[Here's James in his Santy costume! I think he's smiling under that beard!]

I went to San Francisco with the school board and to Dallas and to Florida. I think they liked me so much because of all those costumes Regina had made for me, so I got a lot of fun wearing them, and gave a lot of joy to others, too. All thanks to Regina and her talent. She were a special miracle every day in my life.

One year when we went to Miami, Florida, there was an apartment on the beach that I stayed in. A huge bam! And Crash! And Sizzle hit nearby. I thought Castro had invaded from Cuba, but it was just lighting that hit the transformer! But I always enjoyed those conventions we went to.

When I went to the Dallas convention, I got to see the Goldrings. I had to see them, being that close to Ft. Worth. I stayed with them a couple of days, and visited with Johnny. By that time he was married to Gale Allen, a daughter of a man who worked for Mr. Goldring. He wasn't the same Johnny Goldring that I knew. His wife just tamed the daylights out of that boy. He weren't too happy. That was the last time I got to see Johnny. He died of cancer after having had a fight with two types of cancer and a heart attack.

That's when I became real close to Kathy. Kathy's just like a sister to me. And I know she feels the same. When Mr. Goldring passed she sent me an honorarium obituary pamphlet of his life and what certain people were dear to him. And I was one of those as his "adopted" son. All the Goldring's loved me. And it was the same with me. Like I said before, I could tell what Pete Goldring was thinking before he said it, because we were just that close. The Goldring's claim I was a special miracle in their lives, but I think they were special ones in my life, for me and my family.

[Kathy at twenty (left) and Kathy in her fifties (right)]

One year, I made a covered bus stop bench for the kids to sit and wait for the school bus. And she made a Santy Clause to wave at everyone on the freeway. We won two or three different times. Mr. Stant won a couple of times, too.

So, we had a good fun time. One year they were putting the abbreviations for the dates on something and Lee Lee had used ones Regina had found in an old text. Mr. Redburn said it wasn't right, but Lee Lee showed him the book, and he had to agree, she'd copied it correctly.

One time Lee Lee got in trouble at school. I didn't know anything about it. There was a parent/teacher conference. Lee Lee was threatening to fight another girl, taller than her, over a boy. That time, neither Regina or I could say anything.

Regina said, "Okay, I'll take care of it."

She had a strong talk with Lee Lee at home, so there was no fight. And, of course, the next year, Lee Lee couldn't even stand that boy anymore.

Later in her school years, Lee Lee had a teacher that was talking about Adam and Eve, and he made a remark to her that I didn't like. So I went to the Principal about it. Her very last high school year, they had a baseball game going on all night. Her very best friend was going to go with her.

The next morning a friend of mine called me and said, "James, your car is up at the market. It's got yellow ribbon all around it."

I took off and went up there. I saw the car, but Lee Lee wasn't around. I was about to pass out with worry. Had she been hurt? Was she alive? All kinds of things went through my mind. Then a detective there told me that the car was involved in a road rage incident. They wanted to know where my daughter had been.

I said, "She was with a friend at this all-night baseball game."

Chapter 3

So I told the police where she might be and went with the police. She was with her boyfriend. And she hadn't told us. When we got to the apartment and knocked on the door, I wanted to whip her for lying to me. But the officer told me if I didn't shut up and behave myself, he was going to lock me up, too.

I behaved myself, went home and told Regina what was happening. Then my daughter called me back. I didn't give her much opportunity to talk. I just said, "I'll be up at the station in a little bit." I may have used some bad language. I hope I didn't, but I probably did.

I was determined that she was going to come back home, and she could explain to her mama. I wasn't going to be the go-between. After I left, she called the house again, and she talked to Regina. Regina told her, "If you don't want your daddy to go to jail, you will come back with him."

So when I got up there, she came back home with me without too much of a fuss. She told her mother what happened. She had loaned the car out to somebody. I don't think she even knew him well. But, it was some kid there in Gila Bend, and they all knew of each other, if not each other personally. She wanted to go back to Gila Bend to see her boyfriend's mother. Regina said, "You can do that, and when you're ready, your daddy can come pick you up and bring you home. You're grounded from using the car for a while."

So, I took her back to Gila Bend, she stayed a couple of hours, called me, and I came to pick her up. She wasn't going to be allowed to drive that car for some time. So that was the hardest time we had with Lee Lee in high school. Otherwise, she was a pretty sweet girl and a good girl. Lee Lee was the mascot for four years. Regina made the Gila Monster costume for her, and Lee Lee wore it four years and then donated it to the school. They finally got a new head for it, because the first one was not air-conditioned and open enough. But they used the rest of the costume for years. Lee Lee and Regina used to pick up cans. This helped buy clothes for school.

Ora wasn't no problem in high school. Regina taught Ora how to drive. One day they were coming in with the pickup, and Ora knocked down a tree.

Regina took the wheel and said, "I'll show you how to do this."

She backed up and knocked the other tree down. Yep, she showed Ora how to do it, all right. They thought I wouldn't notice it, because they went out and got duct tape to tape the tree up. But I knew it soon as I got home.

I told you about our Collie, Bob. Well, we had another dog named Fido. He was everybody's buddy. He loved everyone. The dogcatcher came by one day and tried to get him. Regina saw out the window what was happening and called Fido inside. The dogcatcher knocked on the door. He finally left, and Fido was safe.

One year for Christmas, Regina bought me a rifle. That was when we were in Texas. Johnny Goldring went with me to target shoot. A number of times, I barely missed hitting Johnny by two or three feet. For some reason, he wouldn't ever go hunting with me anymore. He said the animals were safe from me, but my friends might be endangered.

In Arizona I went to target practice and I even went deer hunting. I spotted one, shot at it and missed. That deer was safe, too.

[*"I seen the deer, I shot at the deer, the deer turned around and looked at me. I had plenty of time to shoot. . ."*
So this one on the wall was shot by someone else out hunting.]

Now, at Paloma I went deer hunting with a friend of mine. I seen the deer, I shot at the deer, the deer turned around and looked at me. I had plenty of time to shoot again but didn't. From that point on, I had a nickname: Barney Fife. That was the last time I went deer hunting.

Mr. Van Fleet shot a deer and hung my tie on it. When I went out to get it another guy went with me who said he knew the area real good. But, it was way off. We got stuck in a badger hole, got turned around there. So we got lost. So finally Mr. Van Fleet went right to it, got it, and brought the deer home. He hung it up in a tree. Then I took it to a place to have the deer dressed out. After Regina died, I got rid of my rifle. I didn't need no gun, period.

And I didn't want my son-in-laws to have it around, either. So I sold it to a friend of mine.

One time one Christmas party we went to, they went and leased a bus, and we went to a big hotel. I got a bonus at work that year. I got drunk at that party, but I wasn't driving since we had taken the bus, so it was okay. Roberta was with my for that Christmas party.

The next time we had a Christmas party at the office. I got drunk again. That time Regina had to come pick me up and bring me home. My sister-in-law chewed them out for getting me drunk. They didn't have anything to do with it. I got myself drunk, but I was in no condition to fuss with her. She was very protective of me and Regina. She could fuss at me, but no one else could.

If she wanted something done, she'd go tell Regina for me to do it. I never would do anything for my sister-in-law because she was so bossy, but I'd do anything for Regina because she never bossed me. She asked me.

As a dad, I didn't whip the kids. Well, the few times I did, Regina had to be there, because those stubborn kids would never cry "uncle," so she had to be there to decide enough was enough. Most of the discipline problems came as a showdown between them and their mother. But . . . I was going to back their mother regardless of what they said.

If my kids wanted something, they always went to Mama. They didn't go to Daddy. If they wanted money, Daddy didn't have the money. They'd go to Mama, and she'd tell me if it was something they really needed, and if it was, then I'd get the money for them.

Joan, my sister-in-law, lived with us about twenty years or so. She helped take care of the kids. My boss, a Mormon, one time kind of questioned that arrangement, and I told my boss there wasn't nothing going on with my sister-in-law. Then they were okay with her living with us. I wasn't no Mormon. I had tough enough time taking care of one wife, much less two!

When people would come to the house and ask to speak to Mrs. Roberts, Joan would ask, "Which one? The bedroom one or the living room one?"

Some folks didn't know what to think about that. Later years, she moved out for a little while and lived by herself. But when she couldn't manage, we went and got her, and she lived with us again.

Joan never did get married. She had a boy she was crazy about at one time. She was ready for marriage, but he wasn't. He took off for New York. He got killed in New York, and they brought his body back home here and buried him out here at Green Acres. She bought the plot right next to him.

One time she worked in a Half-Way House. And a lot of those people were a little bit nutty. And she sort of picked up some of their ways, and she was kind of whacko.

One time we were driving down in Phoenix , and she wanted out. We not let her out, and she started hitting me. Another time we took her to the county hospital, and they released her. And out in the parking lot, she jumped out of the car. Then she once went to church with her mother and her brother. She said everybody was talking about her and leering. So she threw one of her wild tantrums. She finally ended up in a nursing home because Regina and I couldn't take care of her anymore. Her mother wanted to take care of her, but her mother wasn't physically able to, either.

The first nursing home she entered, they sedated her all the time. Her brother got her out of there, and placed her in a different one. At last, she went into the third one, Highland Manor. While there, Joan had a heart attack. She died on the table, but they brought her back from that. She was in a coma for six months, though. They said, if she had another heart attack, they'd make no heroic efforts to bring her back, since she wasn't in her right mind, and couldn't make that decision for herself.

For six months, Regina took Leeran Smith (her mother) down there so she could brush her daughter's hair and help take care of her. She finally died without waking. When she died, she was buried in the plot she'd bought right next to the man she had loved. So, although he'd gone to New York, he'd not gotten away from her. Joan's mother paid something like $4,000.00 for the funeral, and the headstone had been paid for by Joan when she'd bought the graveside plot.

I served the school board for eight years. I got voted out of office after eight years, but I ran for school board again and won. The second eight years was fine until that last year of the eight. It was a terrible year. One day I called the ambulance. Regina was having problems walking at the house. The paramedics looked at her. She wasn't bleeding or nothing. They said she was all right. They didn't take her temperature, pulse or nothing. Little bitty kids could have done better than they did. Two days later, she had another episode.

My son-in-law said, "Dad, you want me to call the paramedics?"

"No," I said, "I'll call them."

I told the dispatcher, "Don't send out the same ones you sent out before. They didn't do nothing to help her."

The paramedics arrived. Sure enough, it was the same ones. However, we had an appointment with the doctor, and we had a vehicle out there to take her to the doctor and everything. But the paramedics were going to take her to the emergency room to Avondale Hospital.

I got so upset, they called the cops on me, who calmed me down, and told me that I had to calmly go out and tell the paramedics that I'd made other arrangements. I did. But meanwhile my son-in-law wanted to whip them. He wasn't gonna whip nobody. He's a big bluffer. But he was acting tough. So the end result was the cab service took Regina to Buckeye to the doctor's office.

He said to her, "You're going over the hospital right now."

He called Buckeye Rescue Unit. We went to the hospital. She was able to walk inside by herself. It was the last time she walked by herself. She had carbon dioxide poisoning. She got too much bad air in her system, and she couldn't get rid of it and it affected her mind. She knew she was in bad condition, and couldn't make sense. They kept her in Maryvale Hospital for nine days.

Pray.
It causes miracles

Then they put her in a nursing home. That was the hardest thing I'd ever done in my life, having to sign the papers for her to be placed in that facility. That nearly killed me. I cried and cried. And to add to the problems, my bosses told my daughter I had to come back to work, or they were going to have to replace me.

I called one of my boss's wife, and told her to tell him I'd be back soon as I got Regina settled in the nursing home. She stayed in the nursing home about a day and a half. Her tubes fell out of her nose. She was taking Lasix, but she wasn't drinking any water. They put water in front of her, but she didn't know she could pick it up and bring it to her mouth. So, they put her back in Maryvale Hospital again.

This time, while in the hospital, Regina had a dream. In it, an old woman wanted her bones. And in the dream Regina fought, because she didn't want to give up her bones, yet. So, when she got a little better, the doctor

promised to put her in a Rehab on Central right behind Mercado I have to say, they took real good care of her. They really did! I told her, "There's just two choices going here. God will either heal you or not. If he heals you, fine, or He'll take you to Heaven."

The doctors said there was an operation they could do which might help her. And they told her she'd be on life support for a while.

She said, "No."

That was her choice. She was afraid she'd be like her sister, Joan. And, if it was a successful operation, she'd have to revert to a baby state again and have to learn again how to eat, how to comb her hair, and everything. She didn't want to go through that.

My pastor and I had some conversations about the possibility that I might lose her. She talked to the pastor some with me. She said if that happened, she wanted me to get married again.

I said, "Naw. I'm gonna be an old hermit."

She said, "No, you won't be an old hermit. You have too much love in you for that kind of life."

At some point she made me promise I wouldn't drive anymore. It was too dangerous because of me falling asleep at the wheel. I did promise her that. I came up to see her as much as I possibly could. One day Regina went into a coma. I was right there when it happened. So was the doctor. She couldn't follow the instructions of moving her arm or leg when the doctor told her to, but minutes later, when a door slammed or a cart clanged, she'd move. I went on back to work and home. My oldest daughter stayed, but finally went home about 9:00 p.m. A little after that, the hospital called me, and told me to hurry.

When I got there, the staff said, "She tried to hang on until you could get here."

But I couldn't get there in time. She couldn't hang on, and about 10:00 p.m., my wife, Regina, died on February 11,

1996. When I went in to see her, she was all cleaned up and everything. We buried her on February 14, 1996, Valentine's Day. She had a beautiful service. One of the church ladies sang one of the songs Regina had requested to be sung. Another one she wanted, we couldn't find the music for.

My brother-in-law, who'd been through the same thing was there. He was a great comfort to me. But, his wife, didn't want him to get married again. And he never did. He lived alone for the rest of his life. After the funeral, I went back to Paloma and back to work. At Paloma, they gave me a plaque for being on the school board for so many years. I told them those sixteen years wouldn't have happened without Regina's backing and support in so many ways. I gave her and the good Lord the credit for those years of service. I gave them a year's notice that I was going to quit. Worked out okay, considering they were going to go out of business anyway.

Just before she passed away, I had promised Regina I wouldn't drive, but I broke that promise. I have sleep apnea. There was many a time she'd be in the car with me, and she'd see I was asleep, but she claimed I could drive better asleep than I could when I was awake. If another vehicle came along, she'd hit me and wake me up.

I'd said, "Yeah, yeah. I'm fine."

If she didn't think I was, she'd make me pull over. Then she would drive. In about five or ten minutes I'd be wide awake and ready to drive again. We came up to Phoenix quite often to visit her mother. We went to church in Gila Bend every once in a while, but usually we'd wind up in Phoenix. That time she'd chewed folks out for getting me drunk, which they didn't. My children were in Tempe with my mother-in-law, and Regina had told her we'd be there as soon as I sobered up. I don't know if it's true or not, because I have no memory of it, but Regina said I kept telling my sister-in-law, Joan, how beautiful she was. I do not remember falling off the couch. Perhaps it was one of the good little miracles in my life that that was the last time I got drunk.

We had some good, good years together. We were married twenty-nine years, seven months and ten days; a little over ten thousand days. When I was in the Lion's Club, she stood behind me in all the offices I held: Secretary, Treasurer, President, Tale-Twister, so she made me a lion outfit. Whenever we had a special occasion, I'd wear that outfit. She also made banners for the Lion's Club. She also made gifts for Mr. Goldring and the children such as belts, animals, wallet, billfolds and checkbook covers.

There was a special time when my daughter rode the bicycle on this trek. She rode the bicycle up there. And, in my lion costume, I rode the bicycle back. A cop tried to pull me over just about where we were supposed to turn off. I could barely stand up from riding the bike, so no telling what that officer thought. He was worried that I was going to catch my tail in the bicycle chain, but I wasn't. I had hold of my tail. That was another wonderful memory and a sweet miracle of touching many lives that Regina gave me and the community through her sewing skills and imagination.

Of course, I told already about being the Easter Bunny. I passed out candy and balloons and such things such as pens, pencils, erasers. One year when I gave out balloons, the guy helping me ran out of helium, so he ended up having to blow them up. He said he was full of hot air.

One year my wife and the high school kids made Easter Bunny kisses. It was a small plastic and yarn thing that when the sides were squeezed it would open up. It had ears for a bunny. Inside, when you squeezed it, there'd be a

Hershey's kissy. Regina and the high-schoolers made about eight hundred of those bunny kisses. I'd take them down to the lower grades and pass them out. They were a big hit.

After Regina died, I wore the costumes one year, and it was really hard on me. But, I gave out key chains in memory of her. They misspelled Gila Bend on the key chains. They put Gila Beno. I called them up and asked what they wanted to do about it. They told me to keep those, and they also sent the corrected ones. I gave out over eight hundred of those. That was really hard, because I was the wearing the costume she'd made with such love, and which we'd enjoyed so many times in our lives. It was really hard on me. I eventually got rid of the costumes. I wish I hadn't, but Idid. I left Paloma in January 1999.

One more thing, when Regina and I were first married, I forgot her birthday. She never reminded anyone about her birthday. So midnight of her birthday comes, and all of a sudden, she kicks me out of bed.

"Hey," I said, "Why? What happened?"

"You didn't give me a birthday present, that's what happened."

After that, I never did forget her birthday. Never. March 2nd. She was born on March 2, 1946. Nope. Never forgot it again. I always remembered our anniversary date. That was no problem. We married June 29th. Doctor Kenneth who took good care of her, had diagnosed her with that Legionnaires' disease. So whenever she got a cold or something, it would be all foamy. When we go to other hospitals, they tell her it was just white spit, and they couldn't take a culture of that. One time we'd taken her into Maryvale for a hernia operation. They repaired it, but they gave her the wrong medicine that time. She was on oxygen for about three years after that. She became well enough, they thought, to go back to work at a nursing home in Phoenix. One time there, she slipped and fell. She hurt her knee. She went into therapy for a while, and then she got to go back to work again. But, she was again on oxygen. We sued the nursing home that had water on the floor that had caused her to fall, but it didn't do any good. We settled out of court for a mere $300.00.

If Regina had lived for fourteen more days or so, she would have been fifty years old, but as it was, she was forty-nine years young when she passed away from the carbon dioxide poisoning, and being overweight. At one time she weighed four-hundred-and twenty pounds. The doctor was giving her B-12 shots to help her lose weight. Dr. Mena claimed he'd outlive both Regina and her sister Joan because of their weight, but he died before them of a double coronary. Be careful what you say. Your miracles might be cut short.

Never give up on anybody. Miracles happen every day.

I'm glad that Regina lived as long as she did, because during the last years a special miracle happened. She and her daughter made-up after a long time of disagreement. That was a special blessing.

> Every person from your past lives as a shadow in your mind. Good or bad, they all helped you write the story of your life, and shaped the person you are today.
>
> ~Doe Zantamata

Chapter 4

During all these years my oldest daughter Ora had grown up from a babe in my arms to a lovely young woman. Ora

had moved to Phoenix to live with her grandmother. She went into nurse's training. She married a fellow for about six months. We lived in a Mexican community, but hoped she'd marry a white boy, and she did. But, she got divorced from him.

One time she went to California. She didn't tell anybody she was going to California with Albert. She thought she could change his bad ways. Well, she couldn't change him. We had the police looking for her and everything. She called when she got back into town. She wanted her mother and grandmother to clean out her apartment for her, and so they did. There was a picture there of Albert in the nude sitting in a chair. Regina got a lot of fun out of that, threatening Ora she was going to send it to Playboy magazine. She and Albert had Tina, their oldest one, who was in a Beauty Pageant. Regina made her a real pretty outfit.

Tina liked me as the Easter Bunny. April was born later, and tried to eat the Easter Bunny! Then they had A.J. One time Albert went and pushed Regina down. He'd got a gun. My daughter had signed for it or something. He wasn't supposed to have it, because he was on parole from selling drugs. He and Regina got in a struggle, the car keys fell, and Regina put her foot on them. He shoved her, knocked her backwards and got the key. He eventually returned the gun, and they got rid of it. What a miracle that no one was hurt. Albert took an Anger Management class. I have since forgiven him.

Finally over at her uncle's house one day, Ora lost her temper. She realized what kind of person he was, and how her mother had given her good advice, so she apologized to her mother. That made both Regina and me happy. So, Ora and Regina were on good terms when Regina passed.

I remember one story on her, when she was working in a nursing home. The manager on her shift gave her a hard time. It made Regina mad, so she went in and let him know that wasn't right. He'd say, "Calm down, now."

She didn't work there anymore. She couldn't work with her sister, either. Joan came into the picture as a nurse's aide. And she would tell Regina what would need to happen on a shift, and Regina would tell Hazel what would happen, thinking little sister was telling older sister how to do her job. And eventually, they got where they wouldn't talk to each other. And I tried to be peacemaker between them. I talked to both of them.

Regina and Hazel were okay as long as Joan wasn't in the picture. One time we went out joy riding. I was driving, of course, and we got stuck in the sand. I couldn't get out of the sand, so I went for help and knocked on a farmer's door. Just as I was knocking, someone came by and honked a horn at me. It was Regina. She got it out of the sand.

I taught Lee Lee how to drive. That was a disaster, not one of the many miracles. Well, I suppose it was a miracle we both survived. She cannot drive a stick shift. She can drive an automatic okay, but NOT a stick shift.

We went once on a fishing trip. My father-in-law gave me a fifty-cent fishing pole. We were down on the canal. Regina took off in one direction. I dropped my fishing pole into the canal.

When I reached over to get it, I said, "It's not very deep."

I slid off. I got the fishing pole in hand. I got it all right, but . . . I couldn't get out of the canal. My two dogs looked at me, but weren't brave enough to come after me. They went for help. In the mean time, I tried again and again to get up, but that culvert was concrete and slippery. I'd lose my footing and down I'd go in the water again and again.

About the time Regina got there, I pulled myself out. She thought that was funny. She was probably laughing so hard she couldn't have gotten me out, so I guess the fact I was able to on my own meant some little angel was giving me a gentle push and helped with that small miracle of keeping me from drowning in the canal. My billfold and everything else I had on was soaking wet, but, I did save that fishing pole. That seemed real important at the time. Don't know why since I didn't catch no fish with it.

I could tell many, many stories about Regina. I loved her, and I always will, and I miss her...

When Regina would get mad at me and want to fight, I'd just say, "Yes, ma'am, yes, ma'am."

She'd holler back, "You don't mean you agree with me. If you don't mean it, don't say it." She'd get madder.

One year I gave Regina a little wine maker. My mother-in-law thought I was getting it for me, but we never did use it. If we went somewhere, she would stand there and wait for me to open the door for her. She expected me to be a gentleman, no matter how long she had to stand there.

One year for my birthday, I got three, maybe four pecan pies. I ate them all. Not at one time, but I ate them all. My brother-in-law one year gave me a necklace. I didn't mean to, but I hurt his feelings, him and his wife. I thought it was sissy to wear a necklace. I don't now... I got a necklace with a cross on it that I wear.

So, after Regina died, it was nearly three years before I started dating again. Ora fixed me up with a date. I went out. She was a nice lady and everything, but I wasn't serious about her. I just wanted a friend to talk to. She wanted more, so I stopped communication. I wouldn't call her anymore. She was a good lady, but I just wasn't serious about her and didn't care about her in any special way.

Ora and Albert came into the picture as matchmakers. They set me up with another lady, a sort of homeless person, Eileen. At least at the time, she lived alone. Her son had moved and then she became homeless. We went out on one date, but it didn't go all that well. She really just wanted a place to live. My daughter knew I had two extra rooms. Ora invited Eileen to come and live with me. So we made a deal, that for her keep she'd clean the house and do the cooking, and I would eat whatever she cooked. She was a good cook, but when it came time to eat, you had to use a magnifying glass to see the food. It wasn't very much. While Eileen boarded with me, I lost sixty pounds. I give her credit for cooking healthy and for me losing weight and everything.

One day the Superintendent of the school called me up and said he had me on the agenda.

He said, "You might want to come down before the meeting, because this might embarrass you."

I wasn't worried. I knew I hadn't done anything embarrassing on that school board So, I just went on to the school board meeting. And Eileen was at that board meeting, too. Humph.

Eileen was at the board meeting to testify against me. What? Yes, to testify against me who had given her room and board and kept her from being homeless on the street. I told the guy that this sounded like some kind of blackmail. They might as well get it on out on the table, so to speak, because I wasn't going to be blackmailed. I hadn't done anything wrong.

I was ready to take whatever consequences they chose to throw at me. But, I lost my temper. I try not to curse, but I was sure mad. My fellow board members were in shock because they had never seen me lose my temper before.

And Frank said, "I've got written down in my journal that you did this, this and this."

I said, "I don't care what you've got written down in your damn journal. It doesn't make a damn bit of difference what you got wrote down if it's not the truth. I haven't done anything wrong."

He tried to get me thrown out of the board meeting because of my losing my temper. I was a member, not president of the board, at this time. David, the president of the board, wouldn't throw me out. He just asked me to calm down. I did.

But after that, the superintendent and me were never close again. I didn't trust him and his judgment about anything. Regina had never liked him way back to begin with. She tolerated him. One of the reasons, was he once held a meeting and didn't tell me, a member of the board about it. He didn't invite me to the meeting. It was all Spanish-speaking people. She was angry at him, because she said he was discriminating against me, and that wasn't right. She didn't like him. But, he did serve as one of her pall-bearers.

When we got home, I told my brother-in-law and this Eileen that we had to come to some kind of agreement. I told her she had to move. Period. I told her, her mouth and her lifestyle was not going to put me in a compromising position again. So, she left, finally. She was not a miracle in my life, but she was a lesson!

One day I was driving to Phoenix to visit my brother-in-law. I would sometimes fall asleep, but the Lord was with me, and I didn't have no accident or nothing. That angel on my shoulder was working overtime. Each time I made a road trip and got back home safely, was a miracle. I was going to give him notice that I was going to move in with him.

But, Leerun had decided to move to Texas. So now, I was worried about what I would do and where I would live. Of course, he couldn't help it. His mother was sick physically and had Alzheimer's disease. He felt bad about not being able to help me out, but he had to take care of her. He felt especially bad because he had to sometimes tie her down so she wouldn't harm herself or others. His sister came out and got both him and his mother back to Texas. So the sister took care of the mother for a while, and when it got too much for her, she had her daughter to help take care of her grandmother.

At the time, her daughter had three young kids, and she was an RN. We always called her Super Woman. Everything she did, she truly was super at. So, my brother-in-law wasn't in good health either, and he wanted to help as he could, so he sold his place in Phoenix. His nephew came and helped him move. Carolyn came down first and helped him get everything organized. They had a yard sale and everything. Sydney Allen came out. He was in the Richland Hills Police Department. They got a van, and he helped move them back to Ft. Worth.

I was lonely as that old pooch Kathy drew. I was left with no place to go. Just before he left, I met Maria who operated an apartment complex. I went to see my daughter, who was renting from Maria. I had taken flowers to my daughter. This lady came out who was the manager. My daughter introduced us. After I left, I called my daughter and asked if the manager lady was married. She was divorced. I called her and we went out. She loves

Karaoke. So, I took her to a bar with Karaoke that she liked. It was kind of scary to me at first, because I hadn't ever been to too many bars. In my world, bars were where you went to get beat up. But the ones she liked were full of music and pretty happy folks. Maria and I hit it off. We dated several times. We went together about a year.

have enough Courage to trust love one more time.

It came to me the Lord wanted me to take care of her and make her happy. I told the Lord, I'd do my best to make her happy. Whatever it would take, I was gonna make her happy. The Lord had set that burden upon my heart, so I asked her to marry me. I also asked her son, if I could marry his mother. Both of them were shocked.

They asked, "Why?"

I said, "Because I love her, and I want to take care of her."

Both of them gave their blessing. We got married on May 22, 1999, 4:00 p.m., at the Bethany United Methodist Church on seventh and Osborn. We'll have been married 15 years on May 22nd. Her youngest son, Richard, was my best man. Her grandson, Little Richard, gave her away (he just goes by Rich now). We had about a hundred people show up for the ceremony.

[This is a photo me and my beautiful Maria taken in 2004.]

After the wedding, we went to Laughlin for the night, because she had to go back to work the next day. So, that's how I met and married Maria. She had been married seven times. I also have met two of her previous husbands. We like each other enough. One she was married to for ten years, Max. He didn't want to be married, really, and after five years she had a nervous breakdown. At that time he wouldn't divorce her, because he didn't want to be blamed for her having another breakdown. At last they got a divorce, but they were still friends.

After we were married a year, we went to New York. I met number six husband, Bob. We got along real good. The reason they broke up was because he threatened her. He often told her never to cross him, because it'd be dangerous. She became scared of him. So, she divorced Bob. Me, Bob and Max gave her a hard time in New York, kidding wise. We've all kept in communication. Bob is in serious health now, blind and diabetic. He's overweight and can't get around well. He's in a nursing home. Max still lives in Phoenix. He had a little run-in, so he went to jail for a while, but he's out now. He can't be around kids or nothing like that. Still, he's my friend, and always will be my friend. I've got another friend who did the same thing. But . . . he was drunk when he did it. My kids had been around him all his life, and he'd never attempted to do anything like that, but drinking can make people lose their inhibitions and good sense.

Maria and I went over and saw Max once in a while and took him out to eat. He has two sisters that live in town, and they look out after him, too. There's nothing I wouldn't do for Max, and I think there's nothing he wouldn't do for me if the occasion called for it.

There are a number of people I think highly of here in Phoenix. One is James Martin. We're both named James. He's always James number one, and I'm James number two, because he's a year older than I am. His wife died, and we were concerned about him being able to take care of himself. He's in assisted living right now and doing real good. They make sure he takes his medicine like he's supposed to. He has seizures every once in a while, so he can't be out on his own and live by himself. If he has a seizure, there's medical staff right there to take care of him.

We knew he and his wife for about eight years. They were Bingo players. There are several people we're close to here. Daniel Rhodes and his wife, I'm close to them, Johnny Perez and his wife, and others, too. Sue Morris from South Dakota and Richard and Amy LeFebvre. It's homelike and special place to be.

[Another picture of my favorite lady and me taken in 2003.]

And there were others who were a special influence in my life. James Sterling Beloate, my former boss who got me into business college and encouraged me to get a higher education. Mr.

& Mrs. P.A. Goldring, my former bosses, who were my second father and mother. I appreciate all those mentioned and all those not mentioned but in my heart and mind.

Chapter 5

When I first came out to Phoenix from Paloma, I thought it'd be easy for me to get a job doing the same kind of work I did at Paloma. I couldn't find a job right off for about three months. Then I got a job with a Security Company, and after being released from several different posts for different reasons and whatnot, I ended up as a security guard for Wagon Hut. They were at the Motorola by Sky Harbor.

I was there for about two years, something like that. Two years at the same place was sort of a blessing, seeing-as how hard it was to find a job. But . . . they had me on that particular post, and they said I was sleeping on the job. Now, I have sleep apnea, but I don't think I was doing that during the day. Sometimes, I didn't know exactly what was going on, but I didn't believe I was sleeping.

So, they moved me over to the main base. They said they had caught me asleep again, and they called me in. By that time, I was about old enough to draw social security. So I got my Social Security, and then I quit that job in February.

Then I got a job at Safeway sacking groceries. I tell you on that job, they kept me busy all the time. But, about then I had a problem. I went to the doctor with my wife, Maria. I had a colostomy done, and found out that I had colon cancer. So they operated on me.

I told the doctor, "Now remember, Doc, you've got to be number two, not number one...God is number one!"

Everyone was happy with that. What a miracle it was that the disease was found early enough to operate.

They took out eighteen inches of my intestines. When I came to, the doctor said I could go home as soon as I had a bowel movement, to make sure everything was working okay. I remember about that time seeing Scotty, the chaplain at our church. He told me he was going to pray for me.

I said, "Well, pray I can do what's needed to get out of here."

Scotty said, "Praying for someone to break wind is the weirdest prayer I've ever prayed."

So, I did break wind and what-all, and I did get to go home. And, I considered that breaking wind at that point was a small miracle in life, too. Weird, but necessary for healing. In about three weeks, the pills they had given me to sort of knock me out and take away the pain, weren't working. But regardless of what position I laid, the pain was there. But, I got through it all. Despite the pain, I did really well for the first three months of rehab. I went back to work at Safeway. I lasted there three months before I ran out of energy, and I had a relapse. My body wasn't back to completely healed yet.

One day, Maria noticed that I had a knot. Again, a small blessing that she took notice and mentioned it early on. So, I went to the doctor. Sure enough, I had a hernia The lady doctor repaired the hernia, but they put it too low down. So it developed an infection, so she had to go back in and drain out the infection. After she did that, I was okay. That situation could have ended up very differently, but that angel on my shoulder was doing double duty again, and I came through the ordeal.

Then there was another hernia on me, but it was on the other side. So, I had a different doctor do another hernia

operation, but this time, rather than using the gauze which might have been part of the problem with the infection before, this doctor used human skin. That seemed to work better. I still have one more little hernia, but don't have to get it fixed right now. One reason I've not had it done is because I really wanted this last doctor who was at John C. Lincoln to do it, but he's not practicing medicine anymore. I'd had a lot of miracles right in a row. I didn't want to press my luck with my over-worked guardian angel.

My first wife, Regina, had three or four hernia operations, and they had a hard time getting them to hold. The doctors had tried to talk her into stapling her stomach to help with the weight and the hernias, but she never had it done. I don't blame her since after the last hernia operation, it had taken her almost two years to get well because she developed an allergy to the antibiotics they were giving her.

After the hernias, I had a hemorrhoid problem and the doctor operated on me for that. During the operation, they cut into my colon. I needed extra blood, and they didn't have any on hand. They kept me overnight. I came through it okay, with the Lord's help, of course. The miracles are still coming, thank you. Thank you.

Perhaps this is the moment for which you have been created.

Esther 4:14

Sonoma

And, then I had another operation because I couldn't get a good urine flow. The doctor fixed that pretty easy, and I haven't had any more problems with that issue.

I feel like I have had so many miracles in my life that I think God was with me before I was consciously with Him-before I had accepted Him. He had to have been there with me, or I wouldn't have made it as long as I did. I believe He had His hand on me before I realized it.

I was a bully when a kid, then got punched in the nose. I realized I wasn't a bully anymore. I think the Lord had lots of such moments in my life planned to open my eyes, mind, and heart. Over the years my thinking has changed. For example, the way I grew up thinking about women like my Dad did, has changed. I am not the boss of any lady. Wasn't meant to be. Everybody has an equal say, and I learned that by Him sending me Regina and Maria and other decent, strong women into my life.

Psalms
94:19
When doubts filled my mind, your comfort gave me renewed hope and cheer.

When I was twelve years old, I had my eyes operated on. My step-mother and step-sister stayed up and nursed me. If I clawed at my eyes, they'd hold my hands down. They were real live angels watching over me. I just didn't appreciate it then, but I realize now how special they were.

My step-mother took care of me during some hard times. My older sister, who was eighteen, didn't think she owed our step-mother any respect. But, at eleven, my Dad insisted I show respect. And when I was failed in the seventh grade, he encouraged me, instilled ambition in me, so I wouldn't give up. I've had some good and decent people always in my life, cheering for me, although at early ages, I didn't appreciate them sometimes.

I never did think of my sleep apnea as a handicap. I know now it physically was, but God showed me around those problems. I've learned you can't put a limit on what God can do. I was baptized when I was about twelve or thirteen in a Baptist church. The meaning of that ceremony never hit me much. I think then I did it because other people were doing it, so I figured I might as well, not realizing what an amazing thing it was.

My step-mother and her oldest son went to a Pentecostal church. And I went with them, of course. And one night the Spirit hit me. At that moment, you're in a world of your own. You're not aware of the people around you. They Baptize "in the omission of your sin" whereas the Baptists say, "In the name of the Father, the Son, and the Holy Ghost." All three being the same, really.

I have felt the Lord, the Holy Spirit, several times in my lifetime, and there's no other feeling like that. When I'm singing to the Lord, it's awesome. I feel like I'm in tune with life, with others, with Him. Yes, my wife told me I'm not in tune. I know that. I can't carry a note. Nevertheless, I'm in-tune spiritually.

One of the greatest acts the Lord has done for me is to pick out my wives for me. I never did. He did that. He knew who I needed in my life at that time.

One time, when my first wife, Regina and I lived in Texas, she bought her a seventy-five dollar car. She paid for it herself. She was proud of it. I think it was a 1940 old Chevy. One day I was driving it, turned, and misjudged the speed of the car coming in my direction. They hit me and mashed in the whole side of her car. She never let me forget that, but she did forgive me for not paying enough attention and letting it happen. One time she was going to get her car, and I was down in the dumps, so I didn't want to go.

She said, "Well, you can lay here and cover your head up, but I'm going to get a vehicle."

Since she wouldn't let me mope, I uncovered my head, went with her and we bought a pickup. She always gave me hope. Maria always gave me hope. I've been blessed beyond my due. Thank you.

Anyway, through the small incidents of everyday life and the major ones like all the operations I've had, I've been thankful for the Lord being with me.

I'm proud of my children.

When they both got married (the first time with Lee Lee) and (the second one with Ora), they thought they could change those men to something better. But, they learned you don't change people. Lee Lee got a divorce, and she has a boyfriend, David, now.

They won't get married because the laws and such make it so hard on a couple. They are both on Social Security Disability. They would lose a lot of their benefits if they married. In my eyes, because they love and support each other, they are married spiritually, just not by a piece of legal paper by the state. God approves marriages, not the state. This man, David, that Lee Lee has chosen, has proved many times that he loves her, and she loves him. Right now, she has her son living with them, Ducky Duck.

I'm very proud of Lee Lee, and I think the Lord is with her. I think the Lord is blessing her by letting her have David.

Like that old song says, "It is no secret what God can do."

He works in ways above man's state and federal laws. All you can do really is pray to God, believe in Him, and let Him guide you in your actions. Read your Bible, and let God interpret the Bible to you. If you have questions, then pray about those questions. He'll answer.

I know when my oldest daughter, Ora, married her last husband, Muhammad, I was concerned about him. He is now Moses Bandgura, an American citizen. He said he was a Christian. I thought he might be a Muslim. To me, it doesn't make a difference whether your Baptist or Catholic or whatever as long as you meet the priority of believing in Jesus and God, the Father, who sent Jesus down here for our sins. I don't care otherwise, whether you're a Holy Roller or whatever. And I believe that God knows your heart, and knows whether or not you are sincere when you profess to believe or repent for something. No one else really can tell, but He knows.

I look at the whole philosophical religious thing from the viewpoint of my life of miracles. I've had so many in my life, that I believe I have one more in store. When I do die, I believe I will go to Heaven. And it won't be because of something I said or did, it'll be because of God's grace. He said, too, that we'd get a new body in Heaven.

And . . . to tell you the truth . . . I'm looking forward to that new body. Miracles are gifts from God.

I don't know what lays ahead of me for the rest of my life. The first thing I want is for Him to be in my life. The second thing is I wanted Maria to be happy. Anything I could do to make her happy, I would do that, with God's help.

She has seven kids. Three I've never met. Her oldest son, David McDowell, who served in the Army Reserve for about twenty-six years, is more business-like than the other son, Richard McDowell. Both are blood techs. Richard is a Sunday-school teacher and he loves to do comedy skits. He's real good at it. He's had problems in his life, but has always turned to the Lord for help. He believes the same way I do. We all have problems in life. It's how we handle those problems that counts.

I know I've made mistakes. I've tried to learn from them. One time I got a bonus I just blew it, and didn't use it wisely. Nowadays, I owe doctors and hospital bills. I don't worry about it. I turned it over to the Lord, and pay what I can. If he wants me to pay them, He'll provide me a way to pay them. It is not that I don't recognize that I owe them. I do. I owe them. But I can't pay them in full and still live, pay rent, utilities, and food. One of these days He may see fit for me to win the Lotto, and I will immediately pay them.

One of my grandkids told another one, "Don't tell Grandpa you don't believe in God."

And so far, none of my grandchildren have said such a thing. They were raised with Christian ideals and ideas. My children's mother and me both raised our children that way, and the girls have taught my grandchildren those same beliefs. If I do something wrong, I try to own up to it. I thank the Lord for all He has done for me.

I know several people there at Phoenix Manor who are wonderful people. I witness, but I don't talk much about my beliefs just stated. I try to do it by example and how I treat others.

I hope this story can be inspirational to someone who is down or needs help spiritually. I'm physically weak and broke most of the time, but I'm spiritually strong.

At the end of the tapes, James thanked Kathy for doing this transcript for him. But, Kathy feels doing this transcript was a blessing to her.

She says, "Bless you, my brother, James. Keep the miracles coming!" – With great love and respect, Kathy Goldring

Chapter 6

The Bethany United Methodist Church on seventh and Osborn witnessed the marriage of I and Maria at 4:00 p.m.

Maria's fifth husband was Max West. Maria's sixth marriage was to Bob Caldwell whom she had known for many years. But people change and through the years, she became very afraid of him. Maria was a manager at an apartment complex and had a roommate, Carol Lucas. That gave God a chance to work another miracle in my life.

I called Maria for a date to the J Bar where Maria loved to sing Karaoke. I was somewhat concerned as bars were known for places and situations where one could get beaten up. Luckily, that did not happen, and me and Maria dated for a year.

I went to both of her sons' for permission to marry their mother. I wanted the opportunity to make her happy. Hence, the wedding day arrived and a new miracle of years of happiness opened up. Before about a hundred guests, Rich McDowell, Maria's grandson, gave her away at the nuptials. This was truly a sweet miracle of two special people finding each other.

Some time after the time in New York, the roommate, Carol Lucas, passed away. We took this time to make a big change and moved to Phoenix, Arizona. Maria asked if Max could move with us. I did not want her to have to choose between us, and as Max was a perfect gentleman, I said yes.

We lived for some years at apartments at 815 Maryland Street which was owned by Emily and Ken. Maria served as the manager and caretaker for them. We could take our many trips and not have to worry.

One day Maria had a heart attack. I called the apartment owners to explain she had to quit.

They said, "No. Let her rest up and just collect the rent."

Eventually, that became too much. Me and Maria got our things out of storage and moved in with her son, Richard and his wife, Kathy. Then we got an apartment there, too.

We were already on Social Security, and we wanted to apply for disability, too. Two lawyers, Stephanie Lake and her daughter took the case. The mother took Maria's case and got it through. At that point me and Maria could pay her son, Richard, back for all he had done and paid for.

Soon after, the mother lawyer called and said she had won her case. God was good and working the miracles again. Me and Maria moved into two bedrooms across from the auditorium. Sandy, a little Jack Terrier, died a few days before we moved in.

In 2011, I got a birthday gift for Maria, a dog named Nacho. Nacho was a little female that was part Chihuahua and Jack Russell Terrier. She was house broken. She often got mad at me. Humph.

Maria volunteered to cook once a month. She made great breakfast burritos and biscuits with sausage gravy. She and I also were involved with a Bible Study group that played Bingo.

Maria was a special miracle of stamina as she helped me through Colon Cancer, a Hernia, and Prostate Surgery. In appreciation for my sweet, lovely wife, I planned a special celebration for her 65th birthday. Many friends from Phoenix Manor got the ballroom fixed up. Pastor Ryan and his wife came. Friends from the Bethany Methodist Church came. They loved her singing in the church choir. Pastor Jim and his wife from Glendale Church came. The sons, daughters and grandchildren were there, too. We had loads of wonderful food. Two parakeets got out in the morning and added to the excitement. Finally, the manager, Cheryl, climbed up on the tables and cornered them. It was a successful happy birthday!

For some time Maria had issues with driving the car. She did not think she had a problem. Her son David and I took her to the doctor. They explained she was not dumb, just her mind didn't react fast enough to be safe driving for herself or for others. In her bewilderment and anger at the situation she threatened to get even. I finally shoved the keys at her. She didn't try to drive. It was just a security blanket to have hold of the keys.

Later Maria went into rehab where I had a daughter working. Many said I should have placed her in a particular assisted living facility. The social worker, her son and his insurance found a place, but his first wife had been there some twenty-five years ago. I told them no at first. Then I did some thinking and research and thought perhaps things had improved. I got Dr. Loli to write out a statement that Maria could be in that assisted living facility if I and their little support dog, Nacho, could be with her.

So off we went to Desert Sky Assisted Living which became known as "Roach's Heaven". There, the staff folks were in charge of giving her meds and everything else she needed medically such as special treatments. Me and Maria took meals three times a day down in the dining room.

A new creature came into their lives as I bought a Cockatiel to keep Maria company along with Nacho. Her daughter Regina came from Iowa at Christmas to spend time with her mother. I decorated with a tree and lights. She looked forward to her daughter's visit so she could go to church with Maria.

Jean took me and Maria to church once a month. She was a friend of Richard LeFebvre. They'd go out to eat after church. Then for a while Sharon Noll took them to church.

Sometime later Maria had a heart attack in the hospital. She had to do rehab at Bella Vista which was on the other side from our building. Her room had a window to the outside so me and Nacho could visit her through the screen of the open window.

I had to down-size to a smaller apartment, because Maria was not coming out of Bella Vista. So, I hired a moving company to help. It was costly due to the roaches that had to be dealt with.

One of Maria's nurses asked if they could video one of the visits I had with Maria through the window. It ended up as quite a hit on Facebook. The News picked up on its popularity and did an interview with me and Maria. Pastor Joel put the video on Youtube in Texas and New York.

Hospice of the Valley also worked on Maria's case in partnership with Bella Vista. They tested her for the Covid Virus, and she did have it. Me, family and friends continued our window visits.

Maria passed away on August 11, 2020. Her funeral was at Green Acres Funeral Home. Pastor Joel led the service. She is buried at the foot of the grave plot of me and Regina. The marker says she is now singing with the angels. Me and Maria were married twenty-one years.

In January 2021 I got the virus. Michael took me to the hospital and they sent me right home. Michael took me again, and I told them to wait for my daughter, Ora, to pick me up. She took me to her apartment where she and my grandson Desmond took care of me. During the illness there were more battles spiritually than physically. And another miracle at my age and with that illness was a lot, but God's goodness prevailed.

Because of that miracle, I moved back into my own place on August 26, 2020. Thanks to Michael spraying three times, it was the first time in five years the place had been roach free.

Poor Nacho also got sick so there was a visit to the vet and a shot. With lots of meals of hamburger and rice she slowly improved. Michael said that was another miracle.

One more miracle: Last night I got a text from a woman of thirty-one years who wanted a picture of me. I told her I didn't know how to do that. She was a con-artist and sent a picture of her top half. She'd gotten hold of the news story. She tried several times, but I did not give in!

[Although, I, Kathy Goldring, am transcribing this for my adopted brother James, I will type this part mostly in his own words. I will say, I am the one blessed as was my whole family with the addition of James Roberts into our family.]

"Kathy Goldring, God blessed me having you as my adopted sister. I know I have more miracles coming. One of these miracles will be when I die. I will go to Heaven with God's grace. I do not deserve it, but I will take it. God will be in charge of my life. So if I do go to Heaven, it will be God's will." – James Roberts

The End

Made in the USA
Las Vegas, NV
31 July 2024

93204279R00069